PLAY THESE GAMES

PLAY THESE GAMES

101 Delightful Diversions Using Everyday Items

HEATHER SWAIN

A Perigee Book

A PERIGEE BOOK
Published by the Penguin Group
Penguin Group (USA) Inc.
375 Hudson Street, New York, New York 10014, USA
Penguin Group (Canada), 90 Eglinton Avenue East, Suite 700, Toronto, Ontario M4P 2Y3, Canada
(a division of Pearson Penguin Canada Inc.)
Penguin Books Ltd., 80 Strand, London WC2R 0RL, England
Penguin Group Ireland, 25 St. Stephen's Green, Dublin 2, Ireland (a division of Penguin Books Ltd.)
Penguin Group (Australia), 250 Camberwell Road, Camberwell, Victoria 3124, Australia
(a division of Pearson Australia Group Pty. Ltd.)
Penguin Books India Pvt. Ltd., 11 Community Centre, Panchsheel Park, New Delhi—110 017, India
Penguin Group (NZ), 67 Apollo Drive, Rosedale, Auckland 0632, New Zealand
(a division of Pearson New Zealand Ltd.)
Penguin Books (South Africa) (Pty.) Ltd., 24 Sturdee Avenue, Rosebank, Johannesburg 2196, South Africa

Penguin Books Ltd., Registered Offices: 80 Strand, London WC2R 0RL, England

While the author has made every effort to provide accurate telephone numbers and Internet addresses at the time of publication, neither the publisher nor the author assumes any responsibility for errors or for changes that occur after publication. Further, the publisher does not have any control over and does not assume any responsibility for author or third-party websites or their content.

First edition: May 2012

Library of Congress Cataloging-in-Publication Data

Swain, Heather.
 Play these games : 101 delightful diversions using everyday items / Heather Swain.
   p. cm.
 Includes index.
 ISBN 978-0-399-53744-8
 1. Games—Juvenile literature. I. Title.
 GV1203.S837 2012
 790.1'922—dc23
                        2011043875

PRINTED IN THE UNITED STATES OF AMERICA

10 9 8 7 6 5 4 3 2 1

Most Perigee books are available at special quantity discounts for bulk purchases for sales promotions, premiums, fund-raising, or educational use. Special books, or book excerpts, can also be created to fit specific needs. For details, write: Special Markets, Penguin Group (USA) Inc., 375 Hudson Street, New York, New York 10014.

For my brothers, Chris and Jason, and our children
(Clementine, Graham, Ella, Reed, Harrison, Penelope, and Vivienne)
who I hope will love playing games as much as we do.

ACKNOWLEDGMENTS

Special shouts to the people who helped make this book possible:

Mom and Dad, for teaching us to love games and playing with us even when we cheated

Dan, Clementine, and Graham, for playing with me every day

Em, LJ, and Becky, the best teammates ever

Stephanie Kip Rostan, Monika Verma, and the staff at Levine Greenberg Literary Agency, for seeing the big picture with me, then minding all the details

Meg Leder and her crack staff at Perigee, for bringing this book out into the world

CONTENTS

INTRODUCTION

KIDS ARE NATURAL-BORN game players. Ask them to pick up their socks, and they'll whine and cry and act like you demanded them to move boulders. But turn it into a game (who can do it the fastest), and you'll see socks in drawers in no time.

Playing games is the perfect antidote for boredom. We all do it. Whether it's logging on to computer Solitaire instead of working or folding a paper football during a droning lecture or mounting a family board game on a rainy Saturday, games are part of our lives and probably have been since the first cave kid threw a rock and her brother tried to throw one farther. Not all games need to be competitive, though. The cooperative kind can be just as fun (not to mention edifying).

Though you'll find aisles and aisles of games at toy stores—from card games and board games to computer games on handheld gadgets, computers, and home entertainment systems—you can get all the benefits of a good game with everyday objects hanging around your house. If you involve kids in making the games or set them loose and let them try it themselves, they'll be more invested in playing and just might have more fun. Plus, making and playing games at home have some hidden benefits.

Brain Development

When you look closely at games you'll start to see that most of them involve solving a problem—whether it's how to get that tiny ball into a hole thirty feet away or guessing a book title from your sister's crazy arm flapping—your brain is engaged in some heavy-duty thinking. And with active games, your body is working as well. Great educators have realized that games are an excellent way to engage children in learning—but don't tell the kids. Just present them with games and let them figure that out on their own.

Socialization

Any game that involves more than one person involves socializing, whether it's co-operating during a scavenger hunt or competing to see who can get the most balls in a basket. Playing games with kids teaches teamwork, the consequences of cheating, and how to be good sports whether they win or lose. It's not hard to see how those skills make it into the daily lives of kids in the classroom, on play dates, and later in life in the workplace. But like all things we hope to teach our children, learning to cooperate or to compete without being a jerk takes practice. Humans aren't naturally good at losing, so there will be tears, yelling, and cheating, and maybe somebody will even knock over the board, scattering pieces under the couch when she loses a game, but that's okay. The point is, playing games with kids allows them a safe place to practice getting along, following rules, and learning how to be graceful in defeat. So when your kids deserve a technical foul for the fits they're pitching over a game, call it quits for then, but definitely come back to more games later. If you do that enough you'll start to see more mature players coming to the table.

Saving Money

Ask most kids to name a game and they'll talk about something on a screen. I have no problem with video games. In fact I like them. But like most things that kids love, I figure some boundaries are in order, such as making sure computer games are age appropriate and setting time limits. However, video games and the systems we play them on are expensive! Making games out of paper cups and Ping-Pong balls is cheap . . . and I'll be the first to admit that I like saving a buck. Even more, I like engaging my kids in new and different experiences. So maybe we'll play computer games one day, but the next, we'll make a homemade pinball machine out of a box we found on the street corner.

Fun, Fun, Fun!

And finally, let's not forget the biggest, most important reason for playing games with kids: It's a rocking good time! I think of my own childhood playing neighborhood games of Cops and Robbers or Freeze Tag in our backyard with the fireflies or cozy winter nights around board games with my parents or bonding with my grandmother when she taught us to play Hearts. Gaming defines an important part of childhood and the memories of those times will last. So, turn off the TV, unplug the Wii, and start gathering supplies because it's time to play!

HOW TO USE THIS BOOK

A **GOOD GAME** is one that is easy to learn but hard to master. In this book you'll find some games that are competitive, others that are cooperative. There are games for large groups, duos, and a few that can be played alone. Some of these games are reinterpretations of old favorites (such as Friends and Family Go Fish and a felt version of Tic-Tac-Toe), while others are mini versions of arcade super stars (like Shuffle Button, Micro Golf, and the pinball machine). Some I might have even made up (like Hoop Jousting and the Progressive Photo Scavenger Hunt), but that's not to say someone else hasn't made up something similar somewhere along the line.

This book is set up like a craft book, although some games require little to no crafting to play—only objects found around the house and a set of rules—others require several steps to create the playing objects and surfaces. Sections are arranged alphabetically by the principal material (balloons, Ping-Pong balls, craft sticks, felt, paper, etc.), each with a short introduction and quirky facts about the objects used. Within the section, the games are arranged by difficulty, with the simplest games for the youngest children coming first, and the most difficult games for older children coming last. You'll find the number of players needed and a list of materials for each project. Each game also has step-by-step written and pictorial instructions for how to make everything you'll need out of everyday objects. Last, you'll find easy-to-follow guidelines for how to play each game. As a bonus, I've included fun facts about the games and materials sprinkled throughout the text so you can nerd out on the history of Flickerball or learn about the different kinds of catapults medieval marauders used.

On the next few pages, you'll find a complete materials list—you'll use many of these materials several times over. At the end of the book, I've included a glossary of terms for weird things (like chenille stems and C-clamps), so if you don't know what I'm talking about, check there. Finally, I've included an index to help you find the fun waiting inside, so if you're searching for a good two-player game on a rainy day or if you're in need of some new games to spice up a birthday party, you can find the right game quickly.

My hope is that grown-ups will spend some time making and playing games with kids, but also that this book will inspire kids to play games on their own. To that end, I've tried to write the directions so kids who can read can use this book independently. However, parents should be aware that some projects use tools that require adult supervision (for example, utility knives). Even better, I hope you start innovating by changing my games to suit your interests or make up your own games out of things you find in the world. Most of all, I hope you and your children have as much fun as my kids and I have had when you play these games!

MATERIALS LIST

HERE IS A master list of the materials used in this book. I keep a lot of this stuff on hand, much as a cook will keep basic ingredients in a well-stocked pantry. You might find that you look differently at your trash and recycling or offerings in the local dollar store after you start making games—packaging, boxes, bags, food-storage containers, weird little scraps, odds and ends—all make great resources for your own designs.

From Your Arts and Crafts Supplies
chenille stems
colored pencils
construction paper
craft sticks (jumbo)
crayons
glue
markers (washable and permanent)
paintbrush
poster board
poster paints
stickers
tape (masking, transparent, clear
  packing)

From Your Sewing Supplies
buttons
decals (iron-on)
elastic cord (thin round)
embroidery floss

felt
hook-and-loop fastener
  (self-adhesive tape and dots;
  aka Velcro)
pins (straight and safety)
scissors (pinking shears and/or fabric)
sewing needles
thread
thread spools (empty)

From Your Office Supplies
chalk (white)
envelopes
foam board
hole punch
index cards
paper (white)
paper clips
pencils
pushpins

rubber bands (small, medium, and large)
ruler
scissors (paper)
stapler
sticky notes (aka Post-its)
Tyvek envelopes
whiteboard and dry erase markers (or chalkboard and chalk)

From Your Kitchen
aluminum foil
beans (dried) or popcorn (unpopped)
bottle caps (from soda or beer)
canning jar lid rings
chairs
chopsticks (wooden)
drinking straws
egg cartons (empty)
funnel
measuring cups and spoons
mini-marshmallows
paper cups (in various sizes)
paper lunch bags
paper plates
paper towel tubes (empty)
plastic food storage containers
plastic soda bottles (empty)
pumper from a bottle (such as lotion, soap, or shampoo)
rice (uncooked)
rolling pin

shish kebab skewers (wooden or bamboo)
tea tray
toothpicks
wax paper

From Your Laundry Room
bedsheet
clothespins (wooden hinged)
pillowcase

From Your Party Supplies
balloons (round and long)
wrapping paper tubes (empty)

From Your Toolbox
C-clamps
hammer
nails
tape measure
utility knife
wood (scrap)
yardstick

From Your Toy Box
beanbags
marbles
rocket balloons
small toys (little cars, tiny dolls, bouncy balls, etc.)

From Your Closet
belts

dress-up clothes and costumes
panty hose
scarves or bandanas
shoe box
wire hanger

From Your Sports and Outdoor Play Equipment
hula hoops
jump rope
net (such as one for volleyball or
   badminton)
Ping-Pong balls
plastic baseball (aka Wiffle ball)
rubber playground ball (such as one
   for kickball)
sidewalk chalk

tennis balls

Miscellaneous
bell
blindfold
brooms
buckets
cardboard boxes
coins
digital camera
digital photo printer and paper
elastic bandage (aka Ace bandage)
hardcover children's books
photos of friends and family
stopwatch
string
toilet paper tubes (empty)

BALLOONS

SEEMS THAT BALLOONS show up whenever there's a good time to be had—carnivals, parades, celebrations of every kind. They're like your weird friends Jasper and Betty who somehow get invited to every party. They're good for decoration but even better as the centerpiece for this bunch of balloon games.

FACTS ABOUT BALLOONS

- Early balloons were made from dried animal bladders—imagine blowing that up! Now the kinds of balloons we play with are made from latex, which comes from the sap of a rubber tree.
- Ever wonder why helium balloons float but the ones you blow up with your mouth don't? The answer has to do with the weight of what's inside the balloons and the weight of the gases in the air around you. Helium weighs less than the other gases that make up the air because it has fewer electrons, protons, and neutrons. Carbon dioxide (what you exhale when you blow up a balloon) weighs more than most of the gases in the air so those balloons lay on the floor—lazy bums.
- Okay, then why don't those nifty helium party balloons stay up more than a day? That's because latex balloons have microscopic holes in them that are bigger than helium atoms, so the helium leaks out of the holes, which causes the balloons to deflate and sink.
- NASA uses a special kind of balloon made from Stratofilm, a polyethylene (kind of plastic) that can hold helium for up to three weeks in −130°F air. Want one of those? It'll cost you $120,000.

- ◆ Can't get a real-life balloon? Try the virtual world. Game designers like Ninja Kiwi (makers of Bloons and all its iterations) inspired a slew of virtual balloon popping games you can play on computers and smartphones.

LOONY BALLOONS

Here's a great, noncompetitive game good for groups. Especially groups that like to get goofy.

■ ■ ■ **PLAYERS** 3 or more

MATERIALS
■ writing paper ■ pen or pencil ■ scissors ■ balloons (at least 1 for each participant, but more is better)

▶ **Prep Work**

Cut the paper into strips, so that you have 1 strip per balloon. Write a different funny instruction, such as "Bark

like a dog," "Cluck like a chicken and pretend to lay an egg," or "Rub your belly and pat your head while singing the 'Star Spangled Banner'" on each slip of paper.

Roll up the strips and insert 1 into each balloon. Blow up the balloon and tie.

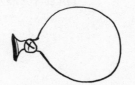

► How to Play

Everyone sits in a circle on the floor. Hand the first balloon to the first person, who bounces on it 3 times. If it pops, the player finds the instruction and follows it, then moves to the outside of the circle.

If the balloon doesn't pop, pass the balloon to the next player who gets 3 bounces, and so on. Continue until all balloons are popped and everyone has had a turn to be silly.

EXTRA FUN

◆ To make it competitive, insert trivia questions into the balloons. The player who gives a wrong answer moves out of the circle until only 1 balloon-bouncing trivia buff is left.

The word loony comes from the word lunatic, which means "to act wildly silly or crazy." This came from the Latin word lunaticus, which meant "moonstruck." In the late fourteenth century, people in the mental health field believed the cycles of the moon affected people's behavior, so the next time you act like a lunatic, tell everyone the moon made you do it.

BALLOON WAITER

Balance balloons on a tray while racing across the floor. The team with the most balloons delivered to the customer wins.

▪▪▪ **PLAYERS** 6 or more

MATERIALS
▪ utility knife* ▪ large cardboard box (at least 12 inches by 18 inches per side) ▪ masking tape ▪ balloons, at least 5 per team

*Utility knives are *very* sharp and should be handled only by adults.

▶ Prep Work

Use a utility knife to cut off the top and bottom flaps of the box. Then cut along the corner seam of each side to separate the box into 4 pieces. Trim 4 pieces to 12 inches by 18 inches.

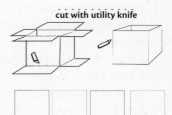

cut with utility knife

Run a line of tape around the edges of each cardboard piece to make them smooth. These are your trays.

Determine your race space. At one end of the space, set up the "kitchen area" for each team that contains the balloons and trays. At the other end of the space, set a chair for each customer.

CUSTOMER AREA

KITCHEN AREA

► How to Play

Divide into equal teams. Each team chooses 1 person to be the customer and 1 person to be the waiter. The others are the kitchen staff.

Seat the customers in the chairs and put the waiters and kitchen staff across from them in the kitchen areas.

The object of the game is to see which team can deliver the most balloons to their customer the quickest while following these important restaurant rules:

CUSTOMER AREA

KITCHEN AREA

1. Only the waiters can move about the restaurant. Kitchen staff must stay in the kitchen area and customers must stay in their seats.
2. Waiters may not touch balloons with their hands. Only the customer and kitchen staff may touch them.
3. Balloons must be delivered by the waiter to the customer on the tray, however this is a respectable establishment and our waiters may use their hands only to carry the tray (that means no pressing the tray up against your tummy to cradle the balloons against your body . . . *quelle horror!*)
4. Any balloon that falls off the tray and touches the ground is no good and cannot be delivered—health department rules.

When the game starts, the kitchen staff must blow up the balloons and tie them.

HELPFUL HINT: Grown-ups may need to help prepare the balloons if young children have trouble blowing up or tying the balloons.

Then the kitchen staff places the balloons on the tray. Next the waiter must transport the balloons to the customer, who may remove them from the tray; but remember, any balloons that touch the ground are no good and cannot be delivered.

Teams will have to try different strategies to get dinner delivered. Is it better to put all the balloons on the tray at the beginning or take them one at a time? How will the waiter best carry the tray—up high, down low? Truly nimble waiters will never let those balloons hit the ground, which might mean some impressive maneuvers with that tray.

Whoever delivers the most balloons, the quickest, wins.

EXTRA FUN

◆ For big groups, make it a relay! Waiters take 1 balloon at a time and return to the kitchen to hand the tray to the next waiter, who must deliver the next course. The team who delivers all the balloons the quickest wins.

Better yet, on a hot day play outside with water balloons.

BALLOON BALL

Batting balloons into boxes brings big belly laughs.

■■■ **PLAYERS** 4 or more

MATERIALS

■ **2 medium cardboard boxes** ■ **construction paper (same colors as the round balloons, such as red and blue)** ■ **glue or tape** ■ **markers** ■ **long balloons* (1 per player)** ■ **2 round balloons of different colors (such as 1 red and 1 blue)** ■ **stopwatch**

*Rocket Balloons (those really big long ones that make a crazy giant angry mosquito noise when you let them go) work great for this game.

▶ Prep Work

Open the top of each box, then cover the sides in the team color. For example, the red team decorates its box with red paper or markers. The blue team decorates its box with blue.

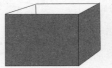

RED TEAM'S BOX **BLUE TEAM'S BOX**

RED TEAM   **BLUE TEAM**

Blow up 1 long balloon for each player and 1 round balloon for each team.

Determine the playing field boundaries. Place 1 box (with the opening facing up) at each end of the playing field.

▶ How to Play

Divide into 2 equal teams. Place round balloons in the center of the playing field. Line teams up in front of their opponents' box, opposite their own box. When the game starts, teams run to the center of the field.

Using only their long balloons, players must pass their round balloon from player to player across the field and into their team's box while following these rules:

1. You may touch the round balloons only with the long balloon. No touching the round balloons with your hands, feet, nose, elbows, arms, tushies, or shoulders. No blowing on the balloon. No willing the balloon to move with mental telepathy. Use only your long balloon. This means you!

2. You must move the ball down the field toward your team's goal by passing it from one player to another using the long balloons. Once a player receives the balloon, he or she can take only 5 steps and then must stop and pass it to another player within 5 seconds. In other words, a single player can't run down the entire field with the round balloon, it must always be passed to another player within 5 steps and 5 seconds. (If you're super serious about this game, you may want to designate an

umpire to enforce the 5-step/5-second rule. Or the players can call each other out when someone's run too far or had the ball for too long.)

Defense with long balloons is allowed. That means you can bat your opponents' balloon away from their team or their team's box.

Once a goal is scored, the action stops. Bring round balloons back to the center and line the teams up at opposite ends again, then resume play.

Play two 5-minute halves. The team with the most points at the end of the game wins.

EXTRA FUN
- For older kids and larger groups, assign a goalie to guard each box. You can also play longer halves or play 4 quarters.
- For a crazy time with lots of players, make 4 teams! Divide into 4 groups. Place a box (each a different color) at each corner of the playing field and 4 round balloons in the center—watch the chaos unfold.

FUN FACT

This game is based on Flickerball, a combination of basketball and football made up at the University of Illinois in 1949 and played by many Midwestern kids during gym class ever since.

BALLOON BATTLE

This classic party game is too good to leave out.

■■■ **PLAYERS** 3 or more

MATERIALS
■ string ■ scissors ■ balloons (1 per player)

▶ Prep Work

For each player, cut a long string (about 2 feet).

Blow up and tie the balloons.

For each player, attach one end of the string to the balloon and the other to the player's ankle.

▶ How to Play

Determine the playing field.

All players line up around the edges of the playing field.

When the game starts everyone runs onto the field. Players try to stomp on each other's balloons to pop them. When a balloon pops, that player is out and leaves the playing field.

The last player with an unpopped balloon wins.

- ◆ If you have lots of players, make teams. Each team is assigned a different color balloon. Teams work collectively to pop other teams' balloons. Last balloon left wins for the team.

ALL ON ONE SIDE

This good, old-fashioned, noncompetitive phys ed game doesn't involve beaning somebody in the head with a rubber ball. It's great for parties and picnics.

■■■ **PLAYERS** 2 or more (but more is better)

MATERIALS
- ■ volleyball or badminton net (or 6- to 8-foot length of rope or clothesline) ■ 1 balloon

▶ **Prep Work**

Set up the net.

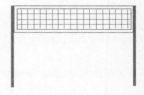

If you don't have a net, play under a clothesline. Don't have a clothesline? Tie a long jump rope between 2 trees or 2 poles.

HELPFUL HINT: Kids, talk a couple of grown-ups into holding the rope at shoulder level 6 to 8 feet apart. You may have to bribe grown-ups to do this. If so, then remind them that as long as you're playing this game, you're not asking them to buy you something. That usually works.

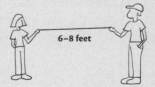

6–8 feet

Blow up the balloon and tie it.

▶ How to Play

Start with everyone on one side of the net. The first player taps the balloon to another player, then slips below the net to the other side.

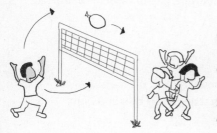

Continue like this until 1 player remains. That player taps the balloon over the net and slips under.

Start again, switching back to the original side of the net.

If the balloon touches the ground, everyone must return to the starting side.

See how many times the whole team can get under the net.

EXTRA FUN
- For really big groups, divide into 2 teams and take turns to see which team can get under the net the most times.

FUN FACT

This game is based on volleyball, an American sport that combines ideas from basketball, baseball, tennis, and handball. The original name for volleyball was mintonette— *sounds fancy, doesn't it?*

INDOOR TENNIS

Get your game on with paper-plate tennis racquets and a balloon ball to bat.

■■■ **PLAYERS** 2 or 4

MATERIALS
- ■ **paper towel tubes (1 per player)** ■ **heavy-duty paper plates (1 per player)** ■ **masking tape** ■ **funnel** ■ **rice (uncooked)** ■ **balloon** ■ **2 chairs** ■ **jump rope (or a 7-foot rope, give or take)** ■ **bedsheet**

▶ Prep Work

To make each racquet, attach a paper towel tube to the back of a paper plate with a long strip of masking tape. Secure the tube with short strips across the back of the plate.

To make the balloon ball, use the funnel to pour 1 tablespoon of rice inside the deflated balloon. Then, blow up the balloon and tie. (The rice makes a cool sizzling noise, but also makes the balloon a little heavier so it's more fun to bat back and forth.)

To make the net, place 2 chairs 5 feet apart in the center of the playing area. Tie a rope from the top of one chair to the top of the other. Lay the sheet over the rope. (Most jump ropes are about 7 feet long, but you can use any size rope; just adjust the net size according to your rope size.)

5 FT

► How to Play

Stand on opposite sides of the net. The first player serves the ball by hitting it across the net. The other player must hit the balloon back again before it touches the ground. If the balloon touches the ground or doesn't make it over the net, the other player scores a point. The first player to 10 wins. Once a server loses a point, switch servers.

You can learn to score like real tennis pros.
  A player must get to 4 points and win by at least 2. The points have funny names:

0 = Love
First point = 15
Second point = 30
Third point = 40
Tie at 40 = Deuce
If server gets the next point after deuce = Ad in
If receiver gets the next point after deuce = Ad out
Final point = Game

  The server always begins by announcing the score, saying her score first, for example, "Love–15," means the server has 0 points and the receiver has scored once. If the score is tied at 15 or 30 the server says, "15 all," or "30 all." If both players have 40, then the server says, "Deuce."
  At deuce, a player must win the next 2 points to

win the game. For example, if the server wins the next point, she announces "Ad in," meaning she has the advantage. If she wins the following point, she wins the game. However, if the receiver wins the point after deuce, then the server announces, "Ad out," meaning the receiver has the advantage. And the receiver must win the next point to win the game. If the game is at "Ad in" and the receiver loses the next point, the score goes back to deuce. Players can go from deuce, to ad in, to ad out, over and over again until 1 player scores 2 points in a row to win the game.

In real tennis, a player must win the majority of 6 games to win a set. So the set score might look like this:

	Game 1	Game 2	Game 3	Game 4	Game 5	Game 6	Total
Player A	X		X	X		X	4
Player B		X			X		2

In this case, the score is 4 games to 2, meaning player A wins the set.

A player must win 2 sets to win the match.

BEANBAGS

THE HUMBLE BEANBAG doesn't get much play anymore, but it's been a member of many toy boxes for centuries. Beanbags are fun to toss because they're soft and easy to catch because they're squishy. You can hide them, collect them, and balance them, too. Here are lots of games to bring back the beanbag!

FACTS ABOUT BEANBAGS

- Beans have been grown all over the world by humans since farming began.
- When combined with a grain, beans form a complete protein, which is important in areas where meat or dairy products such as milk and cheese are scarce.
- The ancient Romans thought beans were so awesome that the most important families named themselves after beans, such as the Fabii (fava bean) family who some claim descended from Hercules, and the Cicero (chickpea) clan whose most famous descendant may have been the Roman lawyer, senator, and philosopher Marcus Tullius Cicero.
- There are thousands of varieties of beans, including Appaloosa beans, azuki beans, turtle beans, brown speckled cow beans, yin yang beans, chili beans, lablab beans, eye of the goat beans, Jackson wonder beans, great white northern beans, rattlesnake beans, and tongues of fire beans.
- When were beanbags invented and who made the first one? Who knows! Surely lots of people put together the idea of stuffing dried beans into a fabric pouch and handing it over to kids to play with.
- Beanbag chairs were invented by Italian designers in 1969 and were originally called Sacco. They were not, however,

filled with beans. Instead they were filled with tiny polystyrene (plastic foam) pellets inside a large pear-shaped leather bag and were meant to conform to the sitter's body.

HOW TO MAKE A BEANBAG

If you don't have beanbags lying around, you can easily make them. Here are 2 DIY beanbag projects, one for sewers and one for those who eschew needle and thread.

HAND-SEWN BEANBAG

MATERIALS
- pinking shears or regular scissors
- square of felt (12 inches by 12 inches)
- ruler
- iron-on decal and iron (optional)
- embroidery floss or strong thread
- sewing needle
- popcorn kernels or dried beans

Use pinking shears to cut two 4-inch by 4-inch squares of felt. Iron the decal onto the center of 1 square if you want, then place the squares on top of one another so that the decal faces up.

Use a strand of embroidery floss to sew the felt layers together, making a seam around 3 sides, ½ inch from the edges. Sew halfway up the fourth side, leaving a long length of floss to complete the last edge later.

Fill the bag with beans or popcorn kernels.

Sew up the rest of the final seam, knot the floss, and cut.

NO-SEW TYVEK BEANBAG

MATERIALS
- Tyvek envelope* - scissors - ruler - permanent makers
- stapler - popcorn kernels or dried beans

*What's Tyvek, you ask? It's the material used to make those strange half-fabric/half-paper mailing envelopes you see at the local office supply store. You'll also find them at the post office in the Priority Mail envelope section, not that you would "borrow" one from the post office to make a beanbag or anything.

Cut out two 4-inch by 4-inch squares of Tyvek. Use permanent markers to draw a picture on one side of each square (if you want), then place the squares on top of one another so that the pictures face out.

Staple the layers together, making a seam around 3 sides, ½ inch from the edges. Make sure the staples are close together so no beans will slip out. Staple halfway up the fourth side.

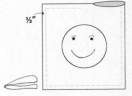

Fill the pouch with beans or popcorn kernels.

Staple up the rest of the final seam.

BEANBAG RELAY

So many silly varieties for teams of 2 or more!

PLAYERS 4 or more

MATERIALS
- 1 beanbag per team

▶ Prep Work

Divide players into 2 or more equal teams. Determine the boundaries of your race space (for example, from the garage to the fence).

▶ How to Play

Line up half the players from each team at one end of the race space and the other half across from them at the other end.

Give 1 beanbag to the first member of each team. Then decide how players will have to transport their beanbags—for example, on top of their heads, on the back of their hands, on the top of their feet, between their knees.

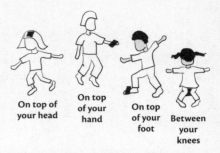

On top of your head

On top of your hand

On top of your foot

Between your knees

Players race from one end of the space to the other and hand off the beanbag to the next player, who races back using the same method. If players drop the beanbags they must stop, replace them, then continue. Teams hand off the beanbag until each member has raced across the space. The first team to get the last member over the finish line wins.

EXTRA FUN

♦ Play again transporting the bags in a different way. Better yet, have players write down on strips of paper all the crazy ways to transport beanbags, then stick the strips in a hat and let the winning team draw the next way you'll race!

FUN FACT

Relay races in which runners handed off a lighted torch started in ancient Greece as a religious ritual held at night, but later this kind of race turned into a sporting event that has been part of the Olympics since 1928.

CORNHOLE

Back in Indiana, we call this game cornhole, but you might know it as a beanbag toss. Whatever you call it, this summer pastime is always fun.

■■■ **PLAYERS** 2 or more

MATERIALS
■ medium-size rectangular cardboard box ■ pencil ■ ruler or yardstick ■ utility knife* ■ poster paints, markers, construction paper, and/or stickers (optional) ■ 4 beanbags of the same color for each player

*Utility knives are *very* sharp and should be handled only by adults.

▶ Prep Work

Use the cardboard box to make a set of target boxes.

Remove the top flaps from your box. Then turn the box on its side so 1 of the long sides faces up and the opening faces toward you. On the side facing up, draw a line from the top left corner to the bottom right corner, bisecting the long side diagonally.

Flip the box over so the opposite side faces up and the opening still faces you. This time, draw a line from the top right corner to the bottom left corner, again bisecting the long side diagonally.

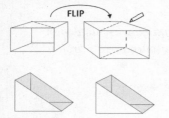

Use the utility knife to cut along the line on one side, then across the bottom of the narrow end, then up the line on the opposite side so that you end up with 2 triangular-shaped boxes.

Set each box on your workspace with the open side down and the flat side facing up so it looks like a ramp. Draw a 6-inch by 6-inch square centered 3 inches from the top. Use a utility knife to cut out the square.

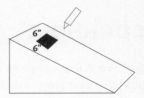

Decorate the target box with construction paper, paint, markers, and/or stickers if you like.

► How to Play

6 feet

Set the target boxes 6 feet (or more) apart with the downward slopes facing inward.

Each player stands beside a target box and takes a turn tossing beanbags toward the opposite box without stepping past the edge of the box.

Beside the box
0 points

On the box
1 point

Inside the hole
3 points

Once each player has tossed 4 bags, add up points as follows: 0 points for bags that land beside the box, 1 point for bags that land on the box, and 3 points for bags that land in the hole.

Switch sides and play another round!

FUN FACT

The American Cornhole Association was founded in Cincinnati, Ohio, and sponsors tournaments around the United States.

PIP, SQUEAK, AND WILBUR

Here's an old-fashioned party game in which teams of 3 compete to run around the circle, through their teammates' archway, and into the center for the prized bag-o-beans.

■■■ PLAYERS   10 or more to make teams of 3 plus 1 leader

MATERIALS

■ beanbags (you will need 1 less bag than the number of teams, so if you have 4 teams, you need 3 bags)   ■ large open space

▶ Prep Work

Decide who will be the leader, then divide the rest of the players into teams of 3. In each team, name one player Pip, one player Squeak, and one player Wilbur.

Arrange the teams of 3 in a large circle and place the beanbags in the center.

▶ How to Play

The leader calls out one of the names, such as "Wilbur!" All the Wilburs in the game run (clockwise) around the outside of the large circle and back to their teams.

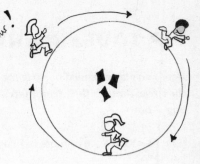

Then Wilbur must pass under an arch Pip and Squeak make with their arms and into the center of the large circle to grab a beanbag.

Wilbur takes the beanbag back to Pip and Squeak and everyone sits down. Each team with a beanbag gets 1 point.

1 POINT

1 POINT

1 POINT

0 POINT

Return the beanbags back to the center of the circle for the next round. Play 5 to 10 rounds. The team with the most points at the end of the game wins.

EXTRA FUN

◆ Use 1 golden beanbag among beanbags of different colors. The team that gets the golden beanbag receives 2 points. Other beanbags are worth 1 point.

TREASURE THIEVES

This super-active game for large groups will instill stealth, trickery, and dishonor—all excellent values for scurvy dogs.

■■■ PLAYERS 3 or more

MATERIALS
■ **chalk or a hula hoop** ■ **1 golden beanbag (doesn't have to be spun from actual gold; it could be made of yellow felt, or maybe it's made of any old color but it has dollar signs drawn on the front and back)** ■ **at least twice the number of beanbags as players (in colors other than the special one)**

▶ Prep Work

If you're outside on a hard surface, draw a small chalk circle (about 3 feet in diameter) in the center of the playing field. Then draw a large chalk circle (about 12 feet in diameter) around the small circle. Or if you're playing on grass or inside, put a hula hoop in the center of the space and set boundaries for the outside of the playing area.

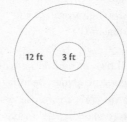

12 ft   3 ft

Place the golden beanbag in the center of the small circle, then pile all the other beanbags on top.

▶ How to Play

The object of this game is to steal the golden beanbag while avoiding being turned into a guard.

Use rock, paper, scissors, or some other nifty way to figure out who will be the guard. The guard stands just outside the small circle to protect the treasure (the pile of beanbags) while the thieves (the other players) spread out around the outside circle.

The thieves run in to steal the treasure without being tagged by the guard. If the guard tags a thief, that thief must return his or her beanbags to the pile and become a guard who helps protect the treasure.

The game ends either when all the thieves have become guards or when a thief gets the golden beanbag. If everyone becomes a guard, then the original guard wins and can choose who will be the guard for the next round (and is allowed to decide to be the guard again).

If a thief gets the golden beanbag, then that person wins and gets to choose who will be the guard.

EXTRA FUN

♦ For a party game played only once, fill a small sealable bag with real treasure (candy, coins, small toys, municipal bonds) and place that at the bottom of the pile. If the guards win, everybody shares. If a thief wins, who knows what will happen?

BEANBAG TAG

Beanbag Toss meet Tag. Tag meet Beanbag Toss.

PLAYERS 3 or more

MATERIALS
- ruler
- belts (or long flat ribbons or strips of sturdy cloth; 1 per player)
- medium-size empty plastic food containers* (1 per player)
- marker
- utility knife**
- beanbags of different colors (5 per player, each player has a different color)

*All of these work well: 32-ounce yogurt container, 1½-quart ice cream container, and 48-ounce disposable round food storage container.

**Utility knives are *very* sharp and should be handled only by adults.

▶ Prep Work

First, you will make a container for each player to
wear around his or her waist. Measure the width
of the belt.

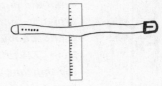

Lay a plastic tub on its side. Make a mark 2
inches from the top. Then use the ruler to draw
a line down the side that is the width of the
belt. Repeat 3 to 5 inches away from the first
line. Cut along these marks with the utility knife.

Slip the belt through the slits in
the container. Attach the belt
around each player's waist so the
container is in the back and the
open side faces up. Give each
player 5 beanbags of a single color.

▶ How to Play

Determine the boundaries of your playing field and how long you want your
inning to be (5 or 10 minutes, or whatever seems right). Tell the players to
spread out around the field.

At the signal, players run around the
field, trying to toss their beanbags
into their opponents' containers
while evading their competitors and
following these rules:

1. If a beanbag lands on the ground when it is tossed, any player may scoop
   it up and use it.

2. Players may not remove beanbags from their containers. If a player falls down, the beanbags that spilled out should be put back into his or her container.

Play for the allotted amount of time, then have everyone sit down to determine the score. First, everyone makes the following 2 piles of beanbags:

1. The beanbags he or she was still carrying at the end of the game (this includes any beanbags that were dropped during play and are still on the ground).
2. All beanbags that are inside his or her container.

Add these 2 numbers together. The player with the *lowest* score wins.

4 + 3 = 7

5 + 0 = 5
WINNER!

RABBIT WARREN

Here's a crafty game (pun!) where you first make masks, then play a tricky game of chase and tag to see which team outsmarts the other.

▪▪▪ **PLAYERS** 6 or more

MATERIALS FOR 6 PLAYERS*
▪ 6 paper plates ▪ pencil ▪ scissors ▪ construction paper (white, pink, and brown) ▪ glue ▪ tape ▪ markers ▪ thin round elastic cord ▪ hole punch ▪ 2 hula hoops ▪ 6 beanbags ▪ 3 scarves or bandanas

*For more players, follow the ratio of materials to players: You'll need 1 beanbag per player, 1 paper plate per player, and half the number of scarves or bandanas as players, but always 2 hula hoops.

▶ Prep Work

First, make 3 rabbit masks and 3 fox masks out of paper plates. Hold a plate up to your face (or a friend's) and gently with a pencil sketch around the eye area. Then make a mark where the tip of your nose touches the plate.

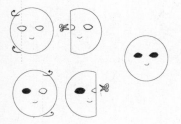

With the plate away from your face, find the center of 1 eye. Fold the plate lengthwise at this point and trim around the eye. Do the same for the other eye. Hold the mask up to your face to make sure the eye holes are in the right place.

Draw a curved line from the nose mark in the center of the plate to either side. Cut along these lines to make the bottom of the animal face.

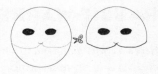

HELPFUL HINT: Cut out the eyes and the bottom of the face on 1 plate and use it as a template for the others by laying it on top of the next plate. Trace around the eye holes and the bottom, then cut. Repeat for all plates.

For 3 of the masks, cut out long floppy ears from white construction paper as well as the interior of the ears from pink paper. Glue the pink paper onto the white paper.

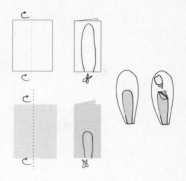

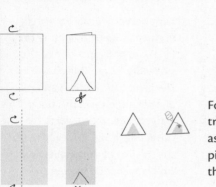

For the other 3 masks, cut out short triangular ears from the brown paper as well as the interior of the ears from pink paper. Glue the pink paper onto the brown paper.

Turn the plates over so the back side faces up and tape the ears onto the tops of the plates.

Flip the plates over and use markers to draw the rest of the faces for each animal.

Hold the elastic at the back of 1 ear, pull it around behind your head to the back of the other ear, and pinch. Snip the elastic where you're pinching. Hold the mask up to your face and make a dot on each side of the mask, just above your ears. Remove the mask from your face and use the hole punch to make a hole at each mark ¼ inch away from the edge. Slip the ends of the elastic through the holes, from the back to the front, and tie small knots.

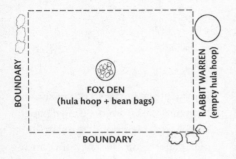

BOUNDARY

FOX DEN
(hula hoop + bean bags)

RABBIT WARREN
(empty hula hoop)

BOUNDARY

Now determine the boundaries of the playing field (your entire backyard or from a tree to the sidewalk). Place 1 hula hoop in the center of the field and put all the beanbags in this hoop. This is the fox den. Next, place the other hula hoop somewhere on the sideline of the playing area. This is the rabbit warren.

▶ How to Play

This is a team game in which the rabbits try to move all the food (beanbags) from the fox den (the hula hoop in the center) to the rabbit warren (the hula hoop on the sideline) before the foxes kill all the rabbits (by pulling off their tails). Brutal, huh? But that's nature for you!

Divide the group into foxes and rabbits and give them the appropriate masks. Also give each rabbit a tail—a scarf to tuck into the back of their waistbands or back pockets. Then have the foxes surround their den and the rabbits surround their warren.

The rabbits then try to steal the foxes' food and the foxes try to kill the rabbits, following these rules:

1. Foxes and rabbits may go anywhere on the playing field.
2. Rabbits are safe from foxes if they crouch down and touch the ground or when they are inside the rabbit warren.
3. Rabbits may stay in a crouched position or in the rabbit warren for only 5 seconds at a time.
4. If a fox pulls a rabbit's tail off (when the rabbit is not touching the ground or in the warren), then the rabbit is dead and must sit out the rest of the game.
5. Foxes may not remove beanbags from the rabbit warren.

If the rabbits successfully move all the food from the foxes' den to the rabbit warren before the foxes slay them all, then the rabbits win. But if the foxes get all the bunny tails before all the food is moved, then the foxes win.

BOOKS

THE OLD SAYING goes, "You can't judge a book by its cover," meaning what's inside counts. That may be true, but in these games, what's inside doesn't matter because the books become building blocks and balancing tools.

FACTS ABOUT BOOKS

- The earliest written documents were made on things such as stone, clay tablets, papyrus, bones, shells, wood, and metal. Actual paper wasn't invented until around the first century AD in China.
- Before printing presses, people called *scribes* carefully copied written documents by hand.
- The first public library was in Athens, Greece, but one of the most famous ancient libraries was the Library of Alexandria in Egypt. It probably housed more than 500,000 volumes. Because the library was destroyed by fire and nothing remained of the books, the only way we know about the Library of Alexandria is by reading about it in other books in other libraries.
- In 1440, Johannes Gutenberg was credited for inventing the printing press, which made it possible to produce lots of copies of books more quickly than by hand. This made books cheaper and easier to get so more people started reading and writing them.
- Early books were not meant for children. It wasn't until the mid-1600s that books for children were made. The first illustrated book for children was called *Orbis Pictus*, an encyclopedia published in Bohemia (now the Czech Republic). Around that same time, a Frenchman named

Charles Perrault started writing down fairy tales (such as "Little Red Riding Hood," "Sleeping Beauty," and "Cinderella") and children's poems and songs, which he called *Tales of Mother Goose*.

◆ eBooks are not as new as you might think. Computer whiz Alan Kay invented the first eBook machine called the Dynabook in 1968! He thought electronic books would be perfect for children. In 1972, he published a research paper about the idea in which he said this kind of book would be "active (like the child) rather than passive." He said it should have "the attention grabbing powers of TV" and that, done correctly, it could be "a tool, a toy, a medium of expression, a source of unending pleasure and delight . . . and, as with most gadgets in unenlightened hands, a terrible drudge!!" Hmmm, sounds a lot like a smartphone, doesn't it?

FINISHING SCHOOL BOOK RACE

It's the oldest race in the book (get it, huh? get it?), and at the end everyone will have excellent posture!

■■■ PLAYERS 2 or more

MATERIALS
- ■ 1 book per racer*

*Flat, hardcover 9½- by 11½-inch children's books work really well.

▶ Prep Work

None.

▶ How to Play

Racers must balance a book on their heads and walk from one end of the race space to the other with their arms at their sides. (No lifting up the arms to catch the book if it starts to slip.) If the book falls off, the racer must stop, pick up the book, reposition it, and then continue.

The first racer to reach the finish line with the book on his head wins!

FUN FACT

In some areas of the world, like West Africa, women and children must walk to a river or well far from home to fill their jugs. To get the water home, they have learned to balance the heavy jugs on top of their heads.

BOOK-BALL-BALANCE RELAY RACE

Teams of 2 balance balls on books.

■■■ **PLAYERS** 4 or more

MATERIALS
- 1 book per player* ■ 1 Ping-Pong ball per team

*Flat, hardcover 9½- by 11½-inch children's books work really well.

▶ Prep Work

Determine the boundaries of your racing space (for example from the tree to the garage).

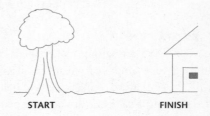

START   FINISH

▶ How to Play

Divide into teams of 2. Give each player 1 book and each team 1 Ping-Pong ball. Then line up the players with the balls at one end of the space and their partners across from them at the other end.

At the signal, players must walk to their partners with the Ping-Pong ball on top of the book, but the book must not touch any part of the body except for hands . . . in other words, no pushing the book up against your tummy to cradle the ball.

If the ball falls off the book, players must stop, replace the ball, and walk forward again.

Once players reach their partners, they must transfer the ball from one book to the other without using their hands except to tilt the book. Then the partner must walk back to the other end of the racing space. The first team to reach the starting position with the ball on the book wins.

EXTRA FUN

◆ For a large group, make it a relay race by dividing into 2 or 3 bigger teams—for example, each team could have 6 players. Half the players line up at one end of the racing space and half at the other. You still need only 2 books and 1 ball per team because players can hand off their books after they've passed the ball to the next player.

NAME THAT BOOK

Readers square off in this TV-game-show-style literary competition.

▪▪▪ **PLAYERS** 3 or more

MATERIALS
- 12 well-known children's books ▪ paper ▪ pencil ▪ bell
- TV tray or small table

► Prep Work

First, decide who will be the host. The host should go through 12 well-known children's book and write down 1 or 2 lines from each story along with the title of the book. Here are some examples:

The Lorax by Dr. Seuss: "But those trees! Those trees! Those Truffalo Trees! All my life I'd been searching for trees such as these."

Where the Wild Things Are by Maurice Sendak: "The night Max wore his wolf suit and made mischief of one kind and another."

Harold and the Purple Crayon by Crockett Johnson: "He made a long straight path so he wouldn't get lost. And he set off on his walk, taking his big purple crayon with him."

Goodnight Moon by Margaret Wise Brown: "In the great green room there was a red balloon."

Green Eggs and Ham by Dr. Seuss: "Could you, would you with a goat?"

Next, set up a bell (the kind people ring when they walk into hotels in old movies) on a TV tray or small table.

► How to Play

Divide players into 2 teams. Have 1 person from each team stand on either side of the TV tray so they are facing each other and the bell is between them. Each player places a hand on the tray, without touching the bell.

The host reads a line from a book, keeping the title and the author a secret. The first player to ring the bell gets to guess the title of the book. If she gets it right, her team gets a point. If she's wrong the other player gets to guess. If he's right, his team gets a point. If he's wrong, the first player can ask for help from her teammates. If they can't come up with the right answer, the other team can guess. Award an extra point if the winning team can also name the author. Then call up 2 new players. The team with the most points at the end of the game wins.

FUN FACT

The first live TV game show was broadcast in England in 1938. It was a fifteen-minute show called Spelling Bee *in which contestants had thirty seconds to correctly spell their word to win a point.*

BOOK-TIONARY

This is a drawing game like Pictionary . . . only with book titles.

■■■ **PLAYERS** 2 or more

MATERIALS
  ■ paper ■ pencil ■ paper bag or hat (or other receptacle)
  ■ white board and dry erase markers (optional) ■ stopwatch or timer (optional)

▶ **Prep Work**

Write down the titles of 10 to 20 well-known children's books or character names on slips of paper, for example, *Little House on the Prairie, Cat in the Hat, Stuart Little,* Harry Potter, and Winnie the Pooh. Then fold the slips of paper in half and drop them into a paper bag.

► How to Play

Players try to guess the title of the book or character from the picture clues drawn by another player. The simplest way to play is to have 1 player (the drawer) pull a slip of paper from the bag then draw clues on the white board or a piece of paper. The other players shout out their guesses as the drawer continues to draw. The first player to guess the correct title or character becomes the next drawer. All players should follow these rules:

1. The drawer may not talk and cannot draw or write letters or numbers as a clue except when a correct word is guessed; then it can be written down.
2. The drawer may, however, draw a blank line for each word in the title and fill in the words as they are guessed. For example, if the title is *Cat in the Hat* the drawer may draw 4 blank lines then write the word *cat* in the first blank once a player says it.
3. Drawers can also use "sounds-like" clues by drawing a picture of an ear and then a picture of something that rhymes with the word. For example, if the title is *Little House on the Prairie*, the drawer might draw an ear and then a head with a lot of hair as a sounds-like clue for *hairy* (rhymes with *prairie*).

EXTRA FUN
◆ Here are 2 ways to play with larger groups:

1. Divide into teams of 2. For each round, 1 player from each duo will draw and 1 will guess (then switch for the next round). One team chooses a

slip of a paper from the bag. Each drawer looks at the paper. Then at the same time, all the drawers begin drawing clues for their partner. The first person to guess correctly wins a point for their team. The team with the most points at the end of the game wins.

2. Divide into 2 teams. Teams take turns letting 1 player choose a slip of paper and draw clues. Only people on that drawer's team may shout answers. Set a timer for 3 minutes to limit the amount of time each team has to guess. If the team hasn't guessed after 3 minutes, the opposing team may try to guess the answer from the existing clues for a point. The team with the most points at the end of the game wins.

FUN FACT

This game is based on an old party game in which players tried to guess what one person was drawing. That game was turned into a board game called Pictionary by Seattle Games in 1985 and is now distributed by Milton Bradley. CBS turned it into a TV game show in 1997, but it lasted for only a year.

BOOK SCAVENGER HUNT

Here is a nerdy twist on a classic scavenger hunt.

PLAYERS 2 or more

MATERIALS
■ 12 children's books ■ paper ■ pencil ■ paper bag or hat (or other receptacle)

▶ Prep Work

Decide who will be the hider and who will be the hunter. The hider first chooses 12 kids books, then writes a clue for each book that will describe the book and where it is hidden in the house. For example, you hide the book *Pinkalicious* in the kitchen cupboard with the flour and the sugar, then write a clue like this:

"Find the place this rosy gal would keep ingredients for her special cupcakes!" Or, you can hide a copy of *There's a Nightmare in My Closet* in a closet and write: "This is the place bad dreams hide in a funny bedtime story!"

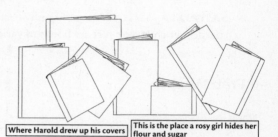

Where Harold drew up his covers

This is the place a rosy girl hides her flour and sugar

The place bad dreams hide

Fold the clues up and put them in the bag and hide the books around the house.

▶ How to Play

If there is more than 1 hunter, they work as a team. One of the hunters picks a clue and reads to the group. The hunters then set off as a team to find the correct book. When that book is found, a different hunter picks out the next clue.

Once all the books have been found, sit down for some quiet reading time!

HOUSE OF BOOKS

This game is like building a house of cards, only with your favorite picture books.

■■■ **PLAYERS** 1 or more

MATERIALS
■ hardcover children's picture books of various sizes

▶ Prep Work

None.

▶ How to Play

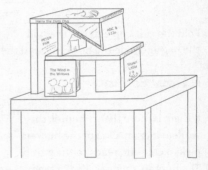

Players take turns placing 1 book at a time on a flat surface to build a house of books. Books can be placed any way you want (upright, flat, open, or closed). You can make it a personal or group challenge to see how high you or a group can build your house of books. Or make it competitive: the first one to knock the house of books over is out, then start over and play again until only 1 player remains.

FUN FACT

U.S. architect Bryan Berg builds enormous free-standing card structures such as re-creations of famous hotels. He used 218,792 cards to build the Venetian (a hotel in Macau).

BUTTONS

I BET YOU'VE been taking buttons for granted, haven't you? There they sit, sewn on your shirt or your pants or your coat, holding everything together, never complaining. Well, there's a lot more to buttons than you might think and here are several games to prove it!

FACTS ABOUT BUTTONS

- Which came first, the button or the buttonhole? Turns out, it was the button. The earliest buttons didn't hold anything closed. Instead, they were worn for decoration during the Bronze Age (about three thousand years ago) and were made from bone, horn, wood, metal, or seashells.
- Nobody got the bright idea for a buttonhole for quite a while after buttons started being worn. The first closure for buttons were loops of thread that went around the button to keep a piece of clothing closed. But then, around 1200 the idea for the buttonhole made it to Europe from the Turks and Mongols who'd solved the ol' button and hole conundrum earlier.
- In 1250, the French Button Makers Guild was established to make beautiful buttons for the aristocracy, who passed laws against peasants wearing them. The royals loved buttons so much that they had to employ professional dressers to help them button up their clothes. King Francis I of France and King Henry VIII of England were both reported to have outfits with more than ten thousand buttons!
- Not everyone loved buttons, though. Church officials in Europe called buttons "the devil's snare," probably because they didn't like women wearing button-fronted dresses.

Later the Puritans declared wearing lots of buttons on a piece of clothing sinful.

♦ The Amish (a religious sect that eschews modernity) does not use buttons because they are considered too showy. Instead, their hand-sewn clothing may be secured with suspenders, zippers, and hook-and-eye closures.

BUTTON, BUTTON, WHO'S GOT THE BUTTON?

This simple game requires exactly 1 button and a room.

■■■ **PLAYERS** 2 or more

MATERIALS
- **1 button**

► Prep Work

None.

► How to Play

The hider stays in the room with the button, while all the other players leave and promise not to peek.

The hider hides the button anywhere in the room and then calls the other players back.

The hider guides the group by saying "cold" when a player is far away from the button, "warm" when a player is getting close, and "hot" when a player is very close, until the button is discovered.

The person who finds the button becomes the hider.

BUTTON CATAPULT

Make a mini-catapult to shoot buttons into an egg-carton target for some tabletop fun.

▪▪▪ PLAYERS 1 or more

MATERIALS

- ▪ empty egg carton ▪ scissors ▪ markers ▪ 1 large rubber band
- ▪ thread spool ▪ jumbo craft stick ▪ 1 small rubber band ▪ ruler
- ▪ masking tape ▪ 10 buttons (various shapes, colors, and sizes)

▶ Prep Work

First you'll make your target. Cut the top off the egg carton and the flap on the front that holds it closed so you have only the section with the egg cups left. Next, write point values in the cups.

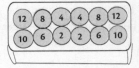

To make the catapult, slip the large rubber band through the center hole of the 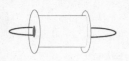 spool so that you have a loop sticking out of either side. (You might need to find something to help you guide the rubber band through the spool, like a chopstick or a knitting needle.)

Turn the spool on its side and lay the craft stick across it perpendicularly (A). While holding 1 rubber band loop steady, pull the other loop up and over the craft stick to the opposite side of the spool then down and around to secure it to the spool (B). Now pull the other loop up and over the craft stick to the opposite side, then down and around to secure (C).

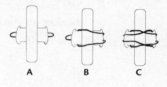

A   B   C

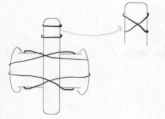

Take the small rubber band and wind it twice 1 inch from the end of the craft stick. Crisscross it underneath the stick and then wind it twice about ¼ inch from the end. Now you have a resting place for your buttons so they won't slide off.

Place a masking tape line 6 inches in front of the egg carton. Put the catapult on the line with the button rest facing the carton and touching the tape.

▶ How to Play

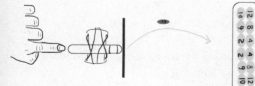

The object is to shoot buttons into the egg carton. Place a button on the rest. Position the catapult along the line to aim it toward the cup you want to hit. Smack the other end of the craft stick to shoot the button in the air toward the egg cups. Add up points for any buttons that land in the cups.

FUN FACT

Catapults were crazy-popular with medieval marauders. They even had different kinds: the ballista worked like a giant crossbow, the trebuchet used a lever and a sling to shoot giant boulders, and the mangonel tossed ammo from a bowl-shaped bucket on the end of a long arm.

BUTTON TOSS

Here's a great game for a party that comes straight from the carnival—without the giant purple panda and the funnel cakes.

■■■ **PLAYERS** Any number

MATERIALS
■ utility knife* ■ medium-size piece of cardboard or foam board ■ markers ■ 2 medium cardboard boxes of the same size ■ masking tape ■ tape measure or yardstick ■ 10 buttons

*Utility knives are *very* sharp and should be handled only by adults.

▶ Prep Work

First, use a utility knife on top of a safe cutting surface to trim your cardboard or foam board to be about 2 feet wide by 4 feet long.

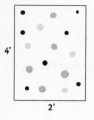

4'

2'

Next, create the game board by drawing lots of polka dots in different colors and in 3 sizes (1 inch, 2 inches, and 3 inches across) on one side of the cardboard.

Balance the game board on top of the boxes (or 2 chairs or on a small table).

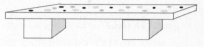

► How to Play

Players line up behind a masking tape line set about 5 feet from the board and then take turns tossing the 10 buttons onto the game board. Then players tally up their points, scoring as follows:

1. buttons that landed on the biggest dots = 1 point
2. buttons that landed on the medium dots = 2 points
3. buttons that landed on the smallest dots = 3 points

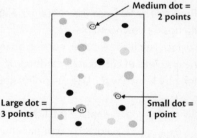

Medium dot = 2 points

Large dot = 3 points

Small dot = 1 point

FUN FACT

Why do we call them polka dots? Polka is a peppy kind of Bohemian folk music and dance that was a craze across Europe and the United States in the early 1800s. Everybody loved to polka! The cheerful, colorful dot design was named after the happy dance.

MONEY IN THE BANK

Here's an excellent game to build hand-eye coordination and addition skills. Or just have fun dropping buttons in a bucket.

■■■ **PLAYERS** 1 or more

MATERIALS
- large empty food container with a lid (as from yogurt or ice cream)
- ruler ■ pencil ■ utility knife* ■ markers, construction paper, stickers (optional) ■ 4 small buttons ■ 4 medium buttons
- 4 large buttons

*Utility knives are *very* sharp and should be handled only by adults.

▶ Prep Work

Remove the lid from the container. Flip the lid upside down and place it on a safe cutting surface (such as a kitchen cutting board or a heavy piece of corrugated cardboard). Measure and mark a rectangle 1½ inches long by ½ inch wide. Use the utility knife to cut out rectangle.

1½" × ½"

Replace the lid on the container. (Decorate the container with construction paper and markers or stickers if you want.) This is the bank.

▶ How to Play

Place the container on the floor. Players take turns standing over the bank, holding one arm shoulder height, and dropping the buttons, 1 at a time, into the slot. Every button that goes in the bank is worth points.

When each player has finished dropping all the buttons, add up his or her score as follows:

1. small buttons = 5 cents
2. medium buttons = 10 cents
3. large buttons = 25 cents

The player who landed the most money in the bank wins!

FUN FACT

Why all the fuss about putting money in the bank? Interest, my friend, interest. Certain banks will pay customers a little bit to keep their money in accounts. This is called **interest***, and it can add up to a lot over many years.*

BUTTON BATTLE

Line up the troops and prepare for battle, Captain Closure.

▪▪▪ PLAYERS 2

MATERIALS
- yardstick ▪ masking tape ▪ 2 large buttons of different colors
- 10 or more smaller buttons (can be different sizes)

▶ Prep Work

To make the playing field, measure an area 24 inches wide by 36 inches long on the floor. Then mark the boundaries of this area with masking tape. Lay a

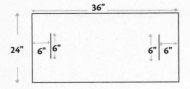

6-inch-long masking tape line, centered 6 inches from each end. These are the firing lines.

How to Play

Give each player 1 large button (the "shooter") and divide the smaller buttons (the "troops") evenly between the 2 players. Players line up their troops between the firing line and the edge of their end of the playing field. Then players place their shooter button on the firing line.

The object is to knock your opponent's troops out of the playing field. Players take turns flicking their shooter buttons toward their opponent's troops. Switch after each flick. Note that the shooter button doesn't have to make it all the way across the field on each flick; in other words, you can use 3 or 4 short flicks to get across. But if your opponent knocks your shooter out of the field, you have to put your shooter back on the firing line.

The shooter must be flicked from the place it lands in the field except:

1. When the shooter button goes out of bounds
2. When 1 of the opponent's troops is knocked out of the field

In either case, the player puts his or her shooter button back on the firing line for the next flick.

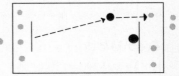

The last player with a troop button (the shooter doesn't count) on the playing fields wins.

BUTTON GOLF

For future pro-golfers who want extra practice at home, here's a version of golf mixed with tiddlywinks, in which you flick buttons into holes made out of toilet paper tube sections. But beware, this game is addictive and infuriating, just like the real thing.

▪▪▪ **PLAYERS** 1 or more

MATERIALS
▪ ruler ▪ pencils ▪ 2 empty toilet paper tubes (or 1 long empty paper towel tube) ▪ foam board or large piece of corrugated cardboard (at least 12 inches by 12 inches) ▪ utility knife*
▪ markers ▪ transparent tape ▪ scissors ▪ white paper
▪ construction paper ▪ 8 toothpicks ▪ masking tape ▪ 1 large button per player (between ¾ and 1 inch in diameter) ▪ 1 small button per player (½ inch in diameter)

*Utility knives are *very* sharp and should be handled only by adults.

▶ Prep Work

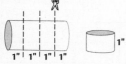

To make the holes, measure, mark, and cut eight 1-inch sections from the toilet paper tubes.

Next, measure and mark eight 3-inch by 3-inch squares on the foam board. Use a utility knife to cut out the squares. For extra fun, color these squares green like grass! Place 1 tube section in the center of each foam board square and attach it with 4 pieces of transparent tape.

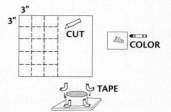

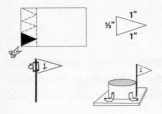

To make a flag for each hole, cut out eight ½-inch by 1-inch by 1-inch triangles from a piece of construction paper. Number each triangle, 1 to 8. Attach the triangles to the top of the toothpicks to make flags. Then poke 1 flag into each piece of foam board, alongside each tube section. Now you have 8 holes, each with a flag, numbered 1 through 8.

For the tee, each player will have a square of foam board from which to shoot. (Um, why not just shoot the buttons off the floor? Glad you asked! You could. But in my endless futzing around with this, I found that the foam board gives the buttons extra zing, which can be key to getting them into the holes, not to mention that it's more fun to watch the buttons pop up high.) To make the tees, measure, mark, and cut out a 6-inch by 6-inch square of foam board for each player.

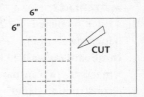

Make a scorecard that looks like this:

Hole	Player 1 Name	Player 2 Name	Player 3 Name
1			
2			
3			
4			
5			
6			
7			
8			

Now comes the fun and creative part! Move the furniture, roll up the rug, and design the course by placing each hole around the room starting with number

1 and ending with number 8. Be forewarned, these buttons can fly! So put each hole at least 2 feet apart. Once you've determined the course, put a loop of masking tape on the bottom of each hole's green and stick it to the floor so it doesn't move during play. Finally, mark the tee line for each hole with a strip of masking tape on the floor. Write the corresponding number on the tape. For example, for the first hole, write a 1 on the tee line tape.

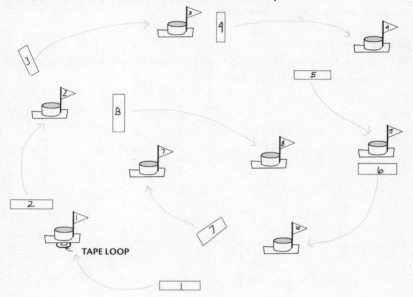

TAPE LOOP

▶ How to Play

Taking turns, players line their tees up with the first tee line and place their small button on the foam board square. Holding the big button between the thumb and the index finger, players aim it toward the hole and press it down against the edge of their little button, making the little button pop up.

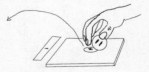

Wherever the little button lands, the player moves the tee to that place, puts the small button on the tee, and shoots again, toward the hole. Count the number of shots it took to get the button in the hole and write this on the scorecard.

HOLE	JOE BOB	BOBBY JOE
1	6	8
2	5	4
3		
4		

The player with the *lowest* score wins!

EXTRA FUN

♦ Design different courses. Add more holes and hazards such as a small bowl of water and wooden blocks.

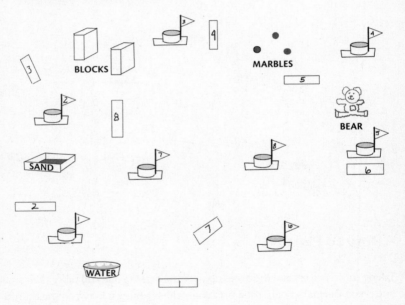

Tiddlywinks (also known as Tiddledy-Winks) has been around since the late 1880s and has taken many forms. The basic idea, though, has always been the same. A player uses a shooter (called a squidger in competitive play) to propel the winks toward a target. Although this game started as nursery play for children, competitive adult tiddlywinks has been around since the 1950s. It continues today with world tournaments, websites, and official rules.

SHUFFLE BUTTON

Create a small, tabletop version of the cruise ship fave, using buttons as pucks.

■■■ **PLAYERS** 2

> **MATERIALS**
> ■ roll of wax paper (12 to 18 inches wide) ■ yardstick or ruler
> ■ foam board or corrugated cardboard (20 inches by 30 inches)
> ■ utility knife* ■ masking tape ■ permanent marker
> ■ 8 (1-inch) buttons (4 of one color and 4 of a different color)
> ■ glue ■ scissors

*Utility knives are *very* sharp and should be handled only by adults.

► Prep Work

Wax paper has 2 sides—the waxy side and the papery side. You can tell by rubbing your thumb and forefinger across the paper. The side that is slick is the

waxy side. The side that feels papery is . . .
you guessed it, the papery side. Remove the
wax paper roll from the box and in a large
open work area, unroll 40 inches of wax
paper with the waxy side facing down and
the papery side facing up.

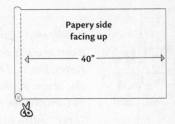

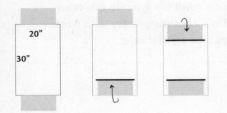

First, use a utility knife on a safe
cutting surface to trim your
cardboard or foam board to 20
inches wide by 30 inches long.
Now, center the foam board on
top of the wax paper. Fold one end
of the wax paper up and over the
edge of the foam board and tape it
to the bottom of the board. Move to the other end of the board. Gently tug the
loose end of the wax paper to make it taut across the board, then fold it up and
over the edge of the board and secure it with tape.

Flip the board over. Now
you have a wax paper
lane in the center of your
board. Use your yardstick
and permanent marker to
draw the following court
diagram on the wax paper.

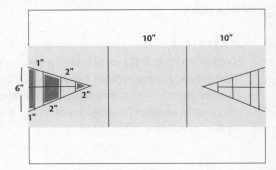

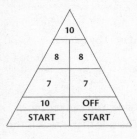

Label each end's triangular scoring area.

To make the pucks, tear off a 4-inch strip of wax paper and lay it waxy side down on your work surface. Flip each button over so that its flat side faces up. Cover this side with glue, then press it down on the papery side of the wax paper. Repeat for 4 buttons in one color, then 4 buttons in the other color. Set aside to dry. Once the glue is dry, cut around each button so that now you have 8 buttons with wax paper glued to their bottoms.

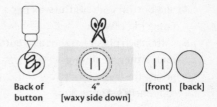

Back of button **4" [waxy side down]** **[front] [back]**

▶ How to Play

Players take turns flicking their buttons (use your forefinger against your thumb to flick) across the court to land in the scoring areas of the opposite triangle.

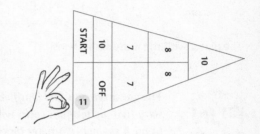

The USA National Shuffleboard Association has all kinds of rules for the competitive version of the game, including lots of penalties for misbehavior on the court. My favorite rule is this: "Players must not talk or make remarks to disconcert opponent's play." Who knew trash talking would be such a problem on the ol' shuffleboard court! Also, the rules stipulate that there will be no smoking on the court during national tournaments, so put away your cigarettes. But I digress. . . . For this tabletop version, we're going to simplify things as follows:

1. Players position 1 button at a time in their own court's start box to begin play.
2. Players take turns flicking their buttons to their opponent's end of the court.
3. You may cause your button to collide with other buttons on the court, knocking them either out of play or into scoring position.

4. If a button goes off the wax paper lane, it is a "dead button" and is no longer in play.

5. After each player has shot all 4 buttons, tally up the score. Buttons count only if they are resting inside the lines of your opponent's scoring area. Also, if your button lands in the "10 Off" area of your opponent, then 10 points will be subtracted from your score.

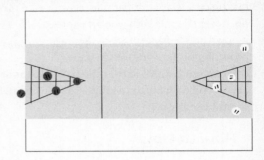

The player with the most points wins!

FUN FACT

The game we now call Shuffleboard is played on a sixty-two- by ten-foot court with a six-foot-long cue to push six-inch-diameter disks from one end to the other. It is popular on cruise ships and in retirement homes, but it started in England in the 1400s and has been called Shove Groat, Slide Groat, Shove-Penny, and Shovel-Penny. It was popular in colonial America.

BUTTON HOCKEY

Air Hockey is an arcade game that manufacturers made smaller so people could play at home. Now you can make your own tabletop version of this classic with just a few things lying around the house.

■■■ **PLAYERS** 2

- large corrugated cardboard box* ■ ruler or yardstick ■ pencil
- utility knife** ■ large sheet of foam board* ■ roll of wax
paper ■ masking tape ■ permanent marker ■ glue ■ scissors
- medium-size buttons (1 to 2 inches in diameter) ■ 2 mini-size
(½-cup, 4-ounce) disposable round plastic food storage containers***
- clear packing tape

*For this project you will slip the foam board inside the box. You will want a box that is at least 24 inches tall by 18 inches wide and a piece of foam board that can be cut to those dimensions.

**Utility knives are *very* sharp and should be handled only by adults.

***GladWare makes a container the correct size.

▶ Prep Work

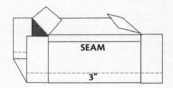

Set your box down the long way with the seam on top. Measure and mark 3 inches up the side from the work surface all around the perimeter of the box (including on the flaps). Then connect these dots with a straight line using your yardstick as a guide.

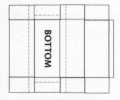

cut with utility knife

Gently pry open the seam on the box and flatten out the box (with the line you just drew face up) on top of a safe cutting surface. Using your yardstick as a guide, cut along the line you drew around the box (including on the flaps) with your utility knife.

The long side of the box now becomes the bottom of your hockey rink. The 3-inch sections will be the sides of the rink. Measure the bottom of the rink, then use your utility knife to trim the foam board to these dimensions.

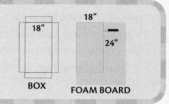

HELPFUL HINT: Cut along the inside of the lines so that your foam board will slide easily but snugly into the bottom of the rink.

Next, cover the foam board with wax paper. Since most wax paper comes in 12-inch rolls, you will use 2 long pieces with a seam down the center of the board. First, unroll a piece of wax paper that is 10 inches longer than your foam board. Lay the waxy side facedown and the papery side faceup on the work surface.

HELPFUL HINT: You can tell which side is which by rubbing your thumb and forefinger across the wax paper. The side that is slick is the waxy side. The other side feels papery.

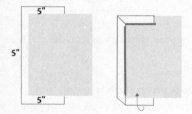

Put your foam board on top of the wax paper so you have 5 inches of paper beyond the ends and one long side of the foam board. Wrap the wax paper up and around the edges of the board and secure with masking tape.

Flip the board over and run a line of clear packing tape along the edge of the wax paper in the center of the board. Then, turn the board upside down again and attach another piece of wax paper to cover the other half of the board.

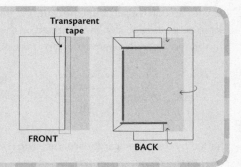

Transparent tape

FRONT

BACK

With the wax-paper-covered side facing up, use a permanent marker to draw the center circle and center line on the rink.

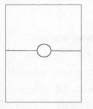

Then draw a straight line across the width of the board.

Now, you will make the goals on either end of the rink. Lay the wax paper–covered foam board with the waxy side faceup in the bottom of the rink. Lift up the flap at the end of the rink so it is flat against the edge of the foam board. Draw a straight line across the inside of the flap where the cardboard meets the foam board.

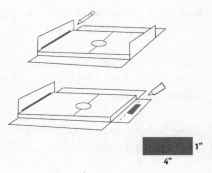

1"

4"

Lay the flap down again, then measure and mark a 4-inch-wide by 1-inch-tall rectangle starting on this line, centered on the flap. Use your utility knife to cut out this rectangle. Repeat on the flap at the other end.

Next, fold up the flaps around the edges of the rink and secure the corners with masking tape. To protect players' arms from getting chaffed by the rough cardboard, run strips of masking tape around the top edges of the rink.

Make the puck by covering the flat side of the button with a layer of glue. Press the gluey side of the button onto the papery side of some wax paper. Allow the glue to dry, then trim the wax paper around the edges of the button.

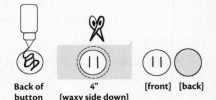

Back of button

4" [waxy side down]

[front] [back]

► How to Play

Give each player one of the little food storage containers without a lid. These will be the puck pushers. Hold the bottom of the container in your hand, turn the container upside down, and place the open end on the rink. It will slide easily across the waxy surface to hit the puck back and forth.

Put the button (wax paper side down) in the center of the rink and yell "Go!" Players hit the puck back and forth to score goals. The first player to 10 wins! Here are the rules:

1. Players can use only their pushers to propel the puck around the rink; no hitting the puck with hands, elbows, toes, etc.

2. Players' pushers may not cross the center line
3. If the puck is on the center line, either player may push it
4. A point is scored if the puck goes through the opponent's goal
5. After a point is scored the player with the puck serves from his or her half of the court

FUN FACT

Real Air Hockey games use a compressor to push air through lots of tiny holes on the playing surface. This reduces the friction (or resistance created when one thing rubs against another) between the puck and the playing surface. This homemade version reduces friction between the button and the foam board by putting a layer of slippery wax paper between them. Clever, huh?

BUTTON BOX

Flick buttons around the playing board in the right order, but don't land in the button box or your button will be sewn on a coat.

■■■ **PLAYERS** 1 or more

*Utility knives are *very* sharp and should be handled only by adults.

▶ Prep Work

First, make the game board. Use a utility knife on top of a safe cutting surface to trim the cardboard into a large square around 2 feet by 2 feet. (But don't sweat the dimensions! If it's a bit bigger or smaller, that's fine.) If the edges of the cardboard are rough, cover them with masking tape.

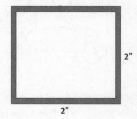

Next, use a marker to draw a 3-inch by 3-inch square in the center of the game board and label it "Button Box" where sad little buttons go before they are sewn onto clothes. This is the no-go zone. Around the edges of the board, draw ten 2-inch by 2-inch squares and number them as shown.

▶ How to Play

The object of the game is to flick a button around the game board from box 1 to box 10 in numerical order, while avoiding the center square and following these rules:

1. Each player gets 1 flick per turn.
2. Players must start with their button in box 1 and shoot for each box in order.

3. As long as the button is on the game board it is fair play and the player can take as many turns as needed to get it into the correct numbered box. (For example, if I'm trying to get from box 2 to box 3 and I accidentally land on box 5 that's okay. On my next turn I flick my button toward 3 again. If I land in the white space between boxes that's okay, too. On my next turn I keep on flicking.)

4. If the button goes off the board, the player must go back to the last box he or she landed in. (For example, if I am going from box 6 to box 7 and shoot my button off the board, I must place it back in box 6 for my next turn and try for 7 again.)

5. If the button lands in the center Button Box, the player must start over at box 1!

6. Players may knock other players' buttons off course, off the board, or into the center square. If a button is knocked off the board by another player, follow rule 4. If a button is knocked into the center square by another player, follow rule number 5.

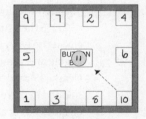

Once a player has landed in each box in the right order (from 1 to 10) the last play is to flick the button in the center square. The first person to do so wins.

In a street-game cousin of this game, kids made their playing board on the sidewalk using chalk and shot bottle caps instead of buttons. They drew a skull and crossbones in the center box, which was called the "dead box."

CARDBOARD BOXES

CARDBOARD BOXES ARE everywhere! And good thing, too, because we have lots of games to play with them. The best part is, when you're done with these games, the boxes can be recycled.

FACTS ABOUT CARDBOARD BOXES

- There are two types of cardboard: paperboard, which is made from layers of paper glued together (like what your favorite cereal comes in), and corrugated board, which has rows of air columns, called the *corrugated medium*, between two flat layers of cardboard called *liners*.
- The corrugated medium (that wavy air column paper between the liners) is made by heating up the paperboard to 212°F then running it through two gear-shaped rollers to give it the wavy look. The wavy paperboard is then covered in glue and pressed between the two layers of liners.
- Nearly 95 percent of all products in the United States are shipped in corrugated cardboard boxes but only 75 percent of those boxes are recycled—a crying shame!
- In September 2009, ION Television created a cardboard box that was approximately sixteen feet by forty-five feet by eight feet in the middle of Times Square in New York City. That box holds the *Guinness Book of World Records* title for the world's largest cardboard box—until someone else comes along and builds a bigger box. So, what are you waiting for? Go set a world record already!

How to Cut Cardboard

1. For flimsy paperboard (such as cereal boxes or shoe boxes), use strong, sharp scissors that are the right size for your hand.
2. When you want to cut a straight line, first draw it on the cardboard using a ruler or yardstick, then cut along the line.
3. Use a utility knife to cut heavier corrugated cardboard (like big cardboard boxes). Remember: Utility knives are *very* sharp and should be handled only by adults.
4. When you want to cut a straight line on corrugated cardboard, lay the ruler or yardstick down and hold if firmly with one hand (making sure your fingertips are out of the way) while you run the utility knife along its edge.
5. Circles are tricky to cut out of cardboard. First, trace a circular object, such as a plate or lid, onto the cardboard. Then use the small sharp tip of the utility knife to cut a square around the circle to get rid of excess cardboard. Finally, work slowly in sections, turning the cardboard as you cut out the circle.

FEELIE-WHATSIE BOX

Good for a party or sleepover!

■■■ **PLAYERS** 1 or more

MATERIALS

■ medium box with a lid (such as a shoe box) ■ lid to a plastic food container ■ pencil ■ utility knife* ■ black felt (12 inches by 12 inches) ■ scissors ■ glue ■ masking tape ■ 5 to 10 small items from around the house (such as a spool of thread, birthday candle, peach pit, and nickel)

*Utility knives are *very* sharp and should be handled only by adults.

▶ Prep Work

Trace the food container lid on the short side of the box.

Use the utility knife to cut out the circle.

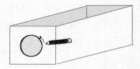

Lay the felt square on the work surface, then put the box on top of it and trace around it. Use scissors to trim the felt to size. Put a layer of glue to cover the inside bottom of the box. Lay the felt on top of the glue and press down.

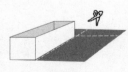

Using the rest of the felt, cut a 4-inch by 4-inch square. From the inside of the box, use masking tape to attach the felt square above the top of the circle so that the other 3 sides are 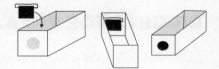 loose. (Adjust the measurements if your box or yogurt lid is smaller or bigger than these measurements.)

Place the small objects inside the box and put the lid on.

HELPFUL HINT: For the youngest players, show all the objects before putting them in the box.

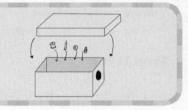

▶ How to Play

One person reaches in through the hole and chooses an object. Before removing the object, the player must guess what the object is. The player then removes the object to see if he or he is right.

EXTRA FUN
- Give each player a turn to find little things around the house to put in the box, then let the other players figure out what's inside.
- This is a great game for theme-based parties. For example, during Halloween tell players the box is filled with ghoulish items like worms (gummy worms), ghost guts (slime), and eyeballs (super balls).

DIGGING FOR TREASURE BOX

Let the archaeologist in you loose on this rice-filled dig.

■■■ **PLAYERS** 1 or more

MATERIALS

■ paper ■ pencil ■ shoe box or see-through food container of the same size ■ 4-pound bag of uncooked rice ■ 12 small objects or toys found around the house (such as a marble, dime, and rubber band)

▶ Prep Work

Make a checklist of the objects you'll use in this game. For prereaders, draw pictures of the objects.

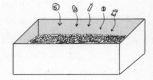

☐ NICKEL 5¢
☐ CANDLE
☐ MARBLE
☐ PAPERCLIP
☐ SPOOL
☐ BEAR ERASER

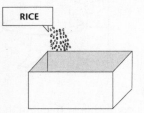

Fill the box three-quarters full with rice.

Drop small objects into the rice and push down to bury them.

► How to Play

Use your hands to take turns sifting through the rice to find the objects. Check each one off as it's found.

HELPFUL HINT: Place the box over spread-out newspaper for easier cleanup in case any rice spills.

EXTRA FUN

◆ Time players to see who can find all of the objects the fastest.

Real archaeologists, scientists who dig for fossils or artifacts from past civilizations, use a variety of tools, such as sifters, shakers, shovels, trowels, and brushes, to carefully extract things from the ground.

BIGFOOT BOX SHOE RACES

Use big box shoes for races and relays.

▪▪▪ **PLAYERS** 2 or more

MATERIALS
- ▪ 2 large empty shoe boxes per player ▪ utility knife* ▪ glue
- ▪ masking tape ▪ paintbrush ▪ poster paint

*Utility knives are *very* sharp and should be handled only by adults.

▶ Prep Work

Cut a semicircular hole in the center of the narrow side of the lid of 1 box. (The size of the hole will depend on the size of the wearer's feet. It should be big enough that the person can easily slip her foot into the opening, but not so big that her foot will come out when walking.)

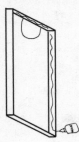

Line the inside rim of the box top with glue.

Put the lid on the box and secure with masking tape around the perimeter where the lid and box meet.

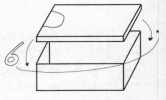

After this dries, decorate the box with poster paint to look like a shoe (such as clown shoes or ballet shoes) or feet (maybe Bigfoot, a monster, or giant smelly human toes).

Repeat for the other foot. Make a set of shoes for each player or team if you're doing a relay.

▶ How to Play

You can either do a race in which every player has his or her own set of big shoes or you can do a relay in which you divide the group into teams of 2 or more and give each team a pair of big shoes.

Determine the start and finish line for your race. Line the players up on the start line and say, "Go!" In a regular race, the first player to cross the finish line wins. In a relay, teammates must put on the shoes before they can race back to the other end of the playing field. The first team to have all players finish the race while wearing the shoes wins.

EXTRA FUN

◆ Design an obstacle course to navigate in those big box shoes!

MINI MARBLE BILLIARDS

Move over, Minnesota Fats! You can practice to be the next big pool shark with this mini billiards table.

■■■ **PLAYERS** 2

MATERIALS

- medium-size rectangular cardboard box* ■ utility knife**
- masking tape ■ yardstick or ruler ■ pencil ■ foam board
- green felt (½ yard) ■ scissors ■ 3 small round stickers
- 16 marbles (1 white; 1 black; 7 of the same color, like blue; 7 of a different color, like green) ■ wooden chopsticks

*Real billiards tables are always twice as long as they are wide, so if you find a box with dimensions that fit this ratio, snatch it up! But for this little version, the dimensions don't matter so much as long as the box is longer than it is wide.

**Utility knives are *very* sharp and should be handled only by adults.

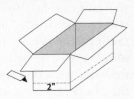

▶ Prep Work

To make the pool table, use a utility knife to trim
the edges of the box so they are 2 inches tall.

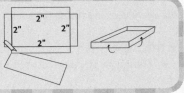

HELPFUL HINT: If you can unfold
your box, this will be easier because
you can cut everything on a flat
surface.

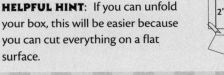

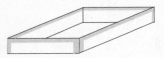

Secure the side seams with masking tape.
Then cover the rough top edges with
masking tape so no little arms get chaffed.

Measure the length and width
of the bottom of your box, then
cut 2 pieces of foam board ¼
inch less than these dimensions.
For example, my box was 14
inches by 26 inches, so I cut my
foam board into two 13¾-inch
by 25¾-inch pieces.

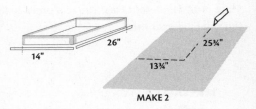

MAKE 2

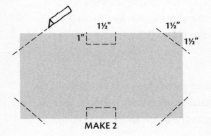

MAKE 2

Next, you will make the pockets. On
each piece of foam board, measure
and mark 1½ inches from each
corner and draw a diagonal line from
one mark to the other. For the side
pockets, from the center point on
the 2 long sides of your foam core,

measure and mark a 1½-inch-wide by 1-inch-tall rectangle. Cut along the lines with a utility knife.

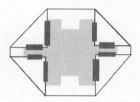

Now you will cover 1 piece of foam board with green felt. Trim the felt so that it is about 1½ inches wider and longer than your foam board.

Center the foam board on the felt. Fold 1 corner of the felt up over the diagonal edge of the foam board and secure with tape. Next, tug the opposite corner so the felt is taut and fold that flap up and over the edge, then secure with tape. Repeat with the other 2 diagonal edges.

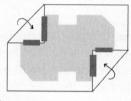

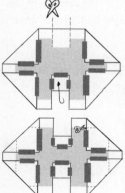

To fold the felt around the side pockets, use scissors to snip the felt at both edges of each side pocket so you create a long, skinny rectangular tab of felt. Fold the tab up and over the edge of the side pocket and secure with tape. Repeat for the other side pocket.

Snip 1 layer of fabric along the dotted lines as shown to avoid bunching.

Fold the remaining flaps of fabric up and over the edges of the foam board and secure with tape.

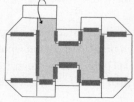

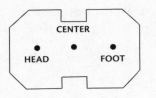

Flip the felt-covered foam board over and place the stickers in the center spot (the exact center of the table), the head spot (halfway between the center spot and one end of the table), and the foot spot (halfway between the center spot and the other end of the table).

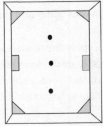

Lay the plain piece of foam in the bottom of the box and top it with the felt-covered foam. This is your pool table.

▶ How to Play

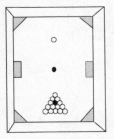

Place the white marble on the head spot (the sticker between the center spot and one end of the table). Then place the other 15 marbles arranged as a triangle with the tip on the foot spot (the other dot between the center spot and the other end of the table) and the black marble (representing the eight ball) in the center of the triangle.

Give each player 1 wooden chopstick to use as a pool cue. To use the cues, stand your pointer finger and middle finger of one hand on the felt (like a little person standing there waiting for something to happen). Hold the end of the cue with the other hand and slide it between the two fingers standing on the felt. This will guide the cue so you shoot straight. Line the cue up with the ball, pull back, then push forward to hit the ball and watch it roll!

To play, flip a coin or say your favorite "you are not it" chant to decide who gets to break. The person who will break also gets to decide which color he or she will play (blue or green, for example). The object is to pocket all of your balls then pocket the black ball before your opponent does.

To break, player 1 hits the white ball toward the triangle to scatter the marbles across the table.

Players take turns hitting the white ball toward his or her marbles, trying to land them in the pockets. (Once a marble lands in a pocket, remove it and set it aside.)

If you pocket a marble, then you get to shoot again.

If the white ball goes into a pocket, it's called a scratch and you lose your turn, plus you have to return 1 of your marbles to the table by placing it on the head or foot spot. And your opponent gets to place the cue ball anywhere on the table before his or her next shot.

If you hit the black ball into a pocket before all of your other balls have been pocketed, then you lose the game, so watch out for that black ball!

MICRO MINI FOOSBALL

Create your own little table soccer game with clothespin shooters and bamboo skewers inside conjoined shoe boxes.

■■■ **PLAYERS** 2

MATERIALS
- 2 adult-size shoe boxes of the same dimensions* ■ utility knife**
- masking tape ■ ruler ■ pencil ■ 12 wooden hinged clothespins (approximately 3 inches long) ■ 6 wooden shish kabob skewers (12 inches long) ■ scissors ■ 12 small rubber bands ■ glue
- black, blue, and red markers ■ 1 marble

*Or any long narrow cardboard boxes that are 6 to 9 inches wide and 12 to 24 inches long.

**Utility knives are *very* sharp and should be handled only by adults.

► Prep Work

After extensive research, I have discovered that shoe boxes come in all shapes, sizes, and varieties of construction—kind of like feet. In other words, I looked at the shoe boxes hanging around my house and realized that they're all different. The trick to this project is finding 2 boxes that are the same width. When I faced this quandary, I walked into a shoe store and asked if the clerk would give me 2 identical empty shoe boxes. She was more than happy to get rid of them.

Once you've got your identical boxes, remove the lids, then open one short side of each box.

HELPFUL HINT: For some boxes you can gently pry up a small flap that folds over the top edge of the short side, then fold down the short side and release the 2 side flaps. If you have an uncooperative box, use a utility knife to slice along the corner seams on one short side per box and then fold the short side down.

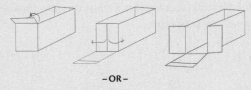

– OR –

No matter which way you opened up the end of your boxes, take 1 box and cut off the short side flap you folded down. This is box A. The other box (with the flap intact) is box B.

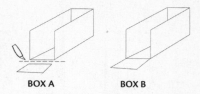

BOX A   BOX B

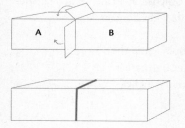

Now, flip the boxes upside down and connect them by placing the open ends together with the flap from box B on top of box A. Run a line of masking tape across the seams on the sides and across the bottom where the boxes join together. Now you should have a box that is 24 inches long.

Next, make the goals at either end of the box. Measure and mark a 2-inch by 1-inch rectangle centered across the bottom of each short side of the box. Then use a utility knife to cut out this rectangle.

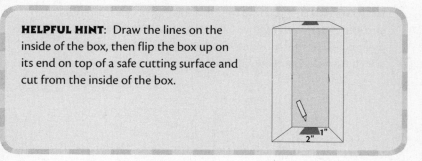

HELPFUL HINT: Draw the lines on the inside of the box, then flip the box up on its end on top of a safe cutting surface and cut from the inside of the box.

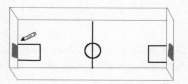

On the inside bottom of the box, draw a line across the center width then draw a circle in the middle. At either end, draw a rectangular goal that is 2½ inches wide by 5 inches long.

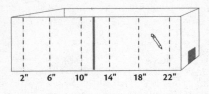

2" 6" 10" 14" 18" 22"

To determine where you will insert the skewers, use a pencil and ruler to draw vertical lines along one long side of the box in the following increments from one end: at 2 inches, at 6 inches, at 10 inches, at 14 inches, at 18 inches, and at 22 inches.

Now, measure from the bottom of the clothespin leg to the small hole (the one between the hinge and the large hole in the jaws). For example, on my clothespin, this is 1⅝ inches.

1⅝"

Measure from the bottom of the box up along the vertical lines this distance plus ⅛ inch (on mine it would be 1⅝ inches + ⅛ inch = 1¾ inches) and make a horizontal mark.

HELPFUL HINT: If you find this befuddling, pay closer attention the next time your math teacher talks about fractions, or ballpark it. The point is, you want to position the skewer so the clothespins hang about ⅛ inch from the bottom of the box.

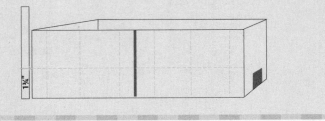

1¾"

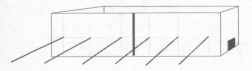

Next, poke a skewer (sharp end first) through the points where the vertical lines meet the horizontal lines.

Push the skewers all the way across the inside of the box so they touch the opposite side. Use your ruler to make sure the skewers are hitting the other side at the same distance from the bottom (1¾ inches on mine) then push the skewer through the opposite side of the box.

Use scissors to snip off the pointy ends of the skewers so no one gets a nasty poke in the palm while playing.

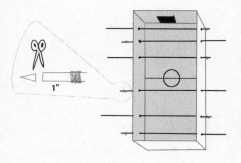

Next, offset the skewers so that every other one sticks out 1 inch from the left side of the box and the other skewers stick out 1 inch from the right side of the box. Wrap 1 rubber band 1 inch from the short end of each skewer (this will stop the skewer from coming out of the holes during heated play).

Next, you will clamp the small holes of the clothespins around the skewers in the pattern shown.

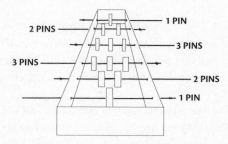

To ensure your clothespins cover the most ground while you're playing, follow these suggestions:

Push the skewers over so that the rubber bands butt up against the sides of the box before you place your clothespins.

For the goalies, align the clothespins with the far side of the goal.

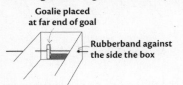

Goalie placed at far end of goal

Rubberband against the side the box

For the 2- and 3-clothespin skewers, make sure the clothespin opposite the rubber bands touches the far side of the box.

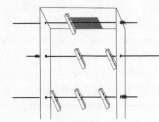

Once you're happy with the position of the clothespins, go back and secure them to the skewer by opening the jaws and placing a small dot of glue on the top and bottom of the hole, then reattach to the skewer. Set aside to dry. This will keep the pins from spinning and moving during play.

For some magical reason, the small hole in the clothespins I used fit precisely over the skewers I used and needed only a bit of glue to stay put. If this is not the case for you, try wrapping a very thin strip of masking tape around the skewer to create the right fit between the skewer and the hole in your clothespin.

Finally, use your red and blue markers to color in the long sides of each skewer so that all the skewers sticking out on the right side of the box are blue and all the skewers sticking out on the left side are the red. This will help players grab the correct skewers during play.

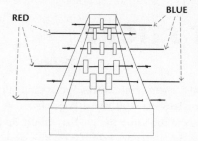

RED   BLUE

▶ How to Play

Players sit on either long side of the box. They control only the 3 long, colored (red or blue) skewers facing them. The object of the game is to defend your goal while trying to hit the ball into the opposite goal to score a point.

Drop the marble into the center circle then spin the skewers to whack the marble into your opponent's goal. Each goal is worth 1 point. The player who is scored upon gets to drop the ball into the center to begin play again. The first player to 10 wins.

FUN FACT

The formal name of this game is table soccer. The word foosball *is from the German word* fuss, *which means "foot."*

CRAFT STICKS

YOU CAN CALL them craft sticks, you can call them tongue depressors, or you can call them Popsicle sticks, but whatever you call them, they're the same thing—flat, round-tip pieces of wood usually made from birch that are great for crafting and game playing.

FACTS ABOUT CRAFT STICKS

- Tongue depressors (that thingie the doctor presses on your tongue when she looks inside your throat) existed during the American Civil War and were made of wood (such as pine) and metal.
- Did you know an eleven-year-old kid named Frank Epperson invented the Popsicle—by accident? He left his fruit-flavored soda outside on a winter day with a stirring stick in the cup. It froze and he knew he had a tasty treat. Originally he called his culinary invention an Epsicle; later his own children renamed it a Popsicle.

STICK TOSS

This is a fun, quiet game of chance that will get you looking for combinations and counting by fives.

■■■ **PLAYERS** 2 or more

MATERIALS
■ marker ■ 3 jumbo craft sticks ■ paper ■ pencil

▶ Prep Work

Use the marker to make dots on one side of each craft stick.

Leave the other side of 2 sticks blank. On the other side of the third stick, draw horizontal lines from the top to the bottom.

Next, make a scorecard like this:

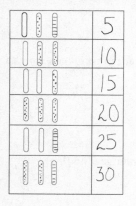

► How to Play

Give players a piece of paper and pencil to keep track of their scores. The first player holds all 3 sticks in one hand and drops them to the ground. Find the combination on the scorecard and write down the score for that round.

Play 5 rounds with players taking turns tossing the sticks and adding up the scores. At the end of the rounds, the person with the highest score wins.

FUN FACT

This game is based on a Native American game called Pa-Tol. Other games, such as Lacrosse, Pick-Up Sticks, Cat's Cradle, and Marbles, are also based on games that Native American children played for centuries.

RING TOSS

Here's a game brought to us by Native American children who knew how to make their own fun with things they found.

■■■ **PLAYERS** 1 or more

MATERIALS

■ string   ■ scissors   ■ jumbo craft stick   ■ canning jar lid ring*

*What, you don't make your own jam? Okay, so neither do I, but I usually have some of these lying around from jars of jam someone else has made. A pack of replacement lids aren't very expensive if you need to buy them. But if that's not your style, you could try bracelets.

▶ Prep Work

Cut a string about 3 feet long.

> **HELPFUL HINT**: Here's a nifty way to measure string without a yardstick or tape measure. Hold one end of the string at the tip of your nose and the other end in one of your hands and stretch your arm out straight to the side. For an average adult, this will be about a yard (which is 3 feet or 36 inches).

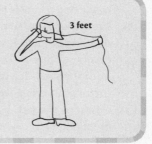
3 feet

Next, use scissors to cut a ½-inch slit in the center of one end of the craft stick. Gently pull one end of the string down into the slit (sort of like flossing your teeth) so that you leave a 2-inch tail sticking out one side of the stick.

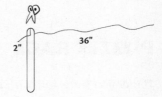
2"   36"

Wrap the other end of the string around the craft stick 3 times and secure it by tying the long end and the tail together in a knot.

Now, tie the other end of the string to the canning jar lid, leaving at least 18 inches of string between the stick and the ring.

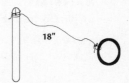
18"

▶ How to Play

Hold the craft stick in one hand and swing your arm to toss the ring in the air, then quickly move the stick to catch the ring.

EXTRA FUN

◆ Make this more of a challenge by cutting a longer piece of string (2 or 3 yards) and tying multiple rings to it, spaced evenly starting at 12 inches from the stick. Try to catch the rings in order, from the closest to the farthest from the stick.

PUZZLE RACE

This project starts with each player drawing a picture across 6 craft sticks that will be turned into a puzzle, then players race to see who can reassemble their own puzzle the quickest.

■■■ **PLAYERS** 2 or more

┌─ **MATERIALS** ───────────────────────
■ **6 jumbo craft sticks per player** ■ **masking tape** ■ **markers**
└────────────────────────────────────

► Prep Work

Make a puzzle for each player by laying 6 craft sticks side by side, then put a long piece of masking tape across the bottom and top of the sticks to hold them together.

Flip the puzzle over so the plain side of the craft sticks is facing up and the tape is facing down. Then have each player use markers to draw a picture across the surface of the sticks.

Remove the tape and mix up the sticks.

► How to Play

Mix together all the craft sticks from all the puzzles and place them in the center of the playing area so that all players can reach them. Say, "Go," and race to see who can complete a puzzle first.

EXTRA FUN

◆ Play alone and see how long it takes to make each puzzle. Or make bigger puzzles using more craft sticks.

WORD RACE

Race to see who can sort sticks into categories the fastest.

■■■ **PLAYERS** 4

MATERIALS
■ 4 index cards ■ 20 craft sticks ■ markers ■ large paper or plastic cup (in which all 20 sticks could fit)

▶ Prep Work

Decide on 4 categories you want to use in this game—for example, animals, fruit, sports, and clothes. Then write each category word on 1 index card and set aside.

FRUIT	ANIMALS
SPORTS	CLOTHES

Divide the craft sticks into groups of 5 with 1 group for each category. On each stick, write a word from the category. For example, for the animals category you could write the words *cat, dog, bear, tiger,* and *chicken*. Then for the fruit category you might write the words *apple, orange, banana, watermelon,* and *grapes*. For sports, *baseball, soccer, swimming, gymnastics,* and *tennis* would work, and for clothes, try *shirt, pants, skirt, socks,* and *hat*.

Put all the sticks together into the cup.

► How to Play

Shuffle the index cards and place them
facedown in the center. Starting with the
youngest player, each person draws a card
to get a category.

One player spills the sticks from the cup
into the center of the circle. Players race
to see who can collect all the sticks in
their category first.

EXTRA FUN

◆ This is a fun early reader or prereader activity that's great for little ones.
   For prereaders, draw pictures or use stickers on the index cards and craft
   sticks for each category.

◆ To make it more challenging, use more craft sticks for each category.

DRESS-UPS

KEEPING A BIG bag of dress-up clothes on hand is great fun for rainy days. Keep old costumes, gather cast-offs from Grandma, raid the thrift stores and yard sales, or just gather a bunch of stuff from all the closets in the house for these super-fun indoor games.

FACTS ABOUT DRESS-UPS

- In the early 1700s, children in wealthy families in America would have worn "stays" under their clothing to promote good posture. Stays were tight-fitting garments buttoned around your torso (the area from your hips to your armpits) with long, straight pieces of bone sewn in to make you stand up straight.
- Think dresses are only for girls? Men have worn skirts and dresses the world over for thousands of years. Ancient Greek philosophers wore togas, and Japanese samurai warriors wore kimonos. Scottish men from the Highlands have been wearing kilts for centuries, and Maasai warriors in East Africa have traditionally worn woven red blankets called *shuka* wrapped around their waists like skirts.

DRESS SHOP

Calling all fashionistas! Here's a fun, noncompetitive game for those who like dressing up.

■■■ **PLAYERS** 3 or more

MATERIALS
  ■ dress-up clothes   ■ 2 rooms

► Prep Work

Put the dress-up clothes in one room and the players in the other room.

► How to Play

Send 1 player into the room with the dress-up clothes to put on a crazy outfit that should include at least 5 different pieces of clothing (shoes, hat, pants, shirt, and vest, for example).

Bring the dresser-upper into the room with the other players, who then study the outfit for 3 minutes.

The dresser-upper goes out and changes 3 things about the outfit and comes back. The players then guess what's different.

FASHION FINDS

Here's a game in which categorizing clothes will result in hilarious outfits to model for one another.

■■■ **PLAYERS** 2 or more

MATERIALS
- ■ dress-up clothes ■ 1 box or bag per player ■ 10 or more index cards ■ markers

▶ **Prep Work**

Divide the dress-up clothes into the boxes or bags so that each player will have lots of choices.

Create a set of at least 10 index cards (or more) with categories that describe things about the dress-up clothes. For example, *blue, hat, pants, red, gloves, frilly*, and *polka dots*. Don't worry about making sure each bag or box has everything on the cards. Part of the fun (or frustration) for players will be finding the items described.

Blue | Frilly | Skirt | Scarf | Boots | Pants | Pink | Glasses | Vest | Polka Dots

▶ How to Play

Give each player a set of dress-ups. Mix up the index cards and turn them upside down. Then choose a card and call out the category. Players dig through their bags to find something that matches the category. By the way, players must put on the items in the order they are read, so if the card with the word *shoes* on it is called before the one with *socks*, then players have to put the socks on over the shoes. And, if any of the players don't have the item called or can't get it on over something already on, then boohoo for them!

After 5 categories (or more if you want) stop. Check out the funny outfits and see who was able to create an outfit with the most items from the categories called.

FOUR CORNERS DRESS-UP GAME

A little racing around, a little matching colors, and a little dressing up add up to a lot of fun.

■■■ **PLAYERS** 4 to 8 players

MATERIALS
- ■ dress-up clothes of many colors ■ 4 medium-size boxes
- ■ construction paper in colors that correspond to the colors of the clothing ■ scissors

▶ **Prep Work**

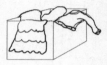

Divide the dress-up clothes into 4 boxes and place one in each corner of the room.

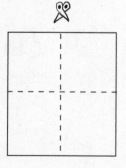

Create color cards by cutting each piece of construction paper into 4 rectangles so you end up with 4 pieces of each (such as 4 blue, 4 orange, and 4 yellow pieces of paper). Mix up the color cards and make a stack.

► How to Play

Have all the players stand in the center of the room. Choose a color card from the stack. Call out the color. Players scatter to any box they want and try to find an article of clothing to match the color.

Draw the next card and call the color. Players must switch boxes and find a new article in the right color. Do this 6 times so everyone is dressed to the nines.

Compare all the funny outfits, then put the clothes back in the boxes and play again!

FELT

BECAUSE MANY OF us don't sew these days, fabric tends to get short shrift as a plaything. But with felt, you can make lots of fun games without ever sewing a stitch. Felt is great because it doesn't unravel, so you can cut it and use it without any hemming. And, just in case you like to sew, there are a few projects that use needle and thread, too.

FACTS ABOUT FELT

- Most fabrics are woven (meaning they are made of interlocking threads woven together side to side and up and down) but felt is different. It's made from matted and compressed fibers.
- The original felt was made by pressing together wool fibers and is probably the oldest kind of fabric in the world.
- One felt legend says that Saint Clement accidentally discovered the felting process by stuffing his sandals with flax and linen fibers and then wandering around until his feet sweated so much that the fibers stuck together, creating fabric. Now, Saint Clement is one of the patron saints for hatmakers, who use a lot of felt in their creations.
- The current-day felt you find in craft stores is most likely made from synthetic fibers (such as polyester and nylon). Nicer felt will also include real wool.

HEARTS AND STARS

Forget about boring old X's and O's in this tactile Tic-Tac-Toe.

■■■ **PLAYERS** 2 players

MATERIALS

■ foam board or corrugated cardboard ■ utility knife* ■ felt squares in many colors (12 inches by 12 inches) ■ scissors ■ masking tape ■ 4 chenille stems (aka pipe cleaners) ■ ruler ■ white chalk

*Utility knives are *very* sharp and should be handled only by adults.

▶ Prep Work

First, use a utility knife on top of a safe cutting surface to trim your cardboard or foam board into a 9-inch by 9-inch square. Next, put the board over the 12-inch by 12-inch square of felt. Snip off the corners of the overhanging fabric. Then fold the flaps of fabric up over the edges of the board, one at a time, and secure them with tape.

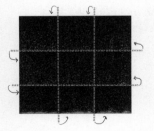

Flip the board over so the felt-covered side is facing up. Lay a chenille stem 3 inches and 6 inches from the left edge and fold the tips over the board to hold the stem in place. Do the same thing with the other 2 stems 3 inches and 6 inches from the top edge to create a 3-by-3 Tic-Tac-Toe grid.

Next, cut another felt square into 3-inch by 3-inch pieces. Fold each piece in half and use white chalk to draw half a heart along the folded edge, then cut out the heart. Repeat 5 times. Do the same with a different color square of felt, only this time make 5 stars.

Or use your imagination to create different kinds of players, such as cars versus trucks, butterflies versus bees, three-headed aliens versus human astronauts!

▶ How to Play

Give 1 player all the hearts and the other player all the stars. Starting with the youngest player, players take turns laying down their pieces on the grid, until someone gets 3 in a row. (You know, Tic-Tac-Toe.)

FUN FACT

Tic-Tac-Toe has been around a long time (maybe since the early Egyptians) and has been called different names around the world, including Wick Wack Woe and Noughts and Crosses.

SEQUENCE SEQUENCE BASIC

Race to re-create patterns in this fun pre-math game.

■■■ **PLAYERS** 2 or more

MATERIALS (FOR 4 PLAYERS)
■ ruler ■ markers ■ large sheet of foam board ■ utility
knife* ■ white chalk ■ 1 black felt square (12 inches by 12 inches)
■ scissors ■ felt squares in 4 different colors (12 inches by 12 inches)
■ masking tape ■ 16 index cards

*Utility knives are *very* sharp and should be handled only by adults.

▶ Prep Work

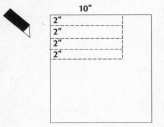

To make the playing boards, measure and mark four 10-inch by 2-inch strips on the foam board. Use the ruler as a guide to cut these strips out with the utility knife on a safe cutting surface (for example, on top of a kitchen cutting board or on top of a heavy piece of corrugated cardboard).

Next, measure and use the chalk to mark four 12-inch by 3-inch strips on the black felt, then cut these out with scissors.

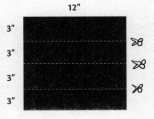

Center 1 of the foam board strips over a black felt strip and snip off the corners of the felt. Then, fold the flap of felt up over the edge of the foam board and secure with a strip of masking tape.

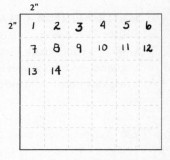

Next, cut out 14 2-inch by 2-inch squares from each color of felt to make heart, square, triangle, and rectangle playing pieces in each color.

Now create 4 of each shape in each color. Use the chart to help you:

Shape	Red	Blue	Yellow	Green
♥	4	4	4	4
■	4	4	4	4
▲	4	4	4	4
▮	4	4	4	4

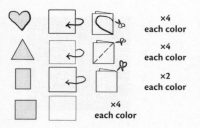

You could make any shapes you want. I've chosen these because they are the easiest to cut out. To make the hearts, fold each piece in half, draw half a heart along the folded edge, then cut. Do the same for the triangles. For the squares, do nothing. For the rectangles, cut 2 squares in half. When you are done, you will have enough for each player to have a set of each shape in each color.

To make the sequence cards, draw each shape in each color on a separate card. For example, a red heart, a blue heart, a yellow heart, and a green heart, a red square, a blue square, a yellow square, and a green square.

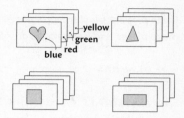

▶ How to Play

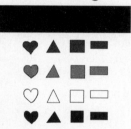

Give each player a board and a set of shapes (everyone should have 1 of each shape in each color).

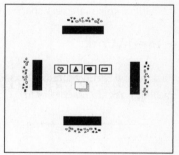

Mix up the sequence cards and place facedown in the center. Starting with the youngest, each player chooses a card and lays it faceup in the center. When there are 4 cards in the center, this is the sequence.

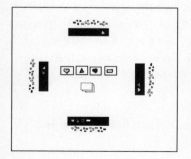

Now, everyone races to re-create the sequence using the felt shapes on their board. The first person to make the sequence wins! Play again.

To make this more challenging, make longer sequences by laying out more cards.

SEQUENCE SEQUENCE SUPER

Once players master Sequence Sequence Basic (on page 107), step it up with more pieces and homemade dice for a bigger challenge!

■■■ **PLAYERS** 2 or more players

*Utility knives are *very* sharp and should be handled only by adults.

▶ Prep Work

First, follow the instructions in Sequence Sequence Basic (page **107**) to create a playing board for each player.

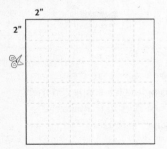

In this game, each player will need 4 of each shape in each color (16 total shapes). To do this, measure and mark a 6-row by 6-column grid on each piece of colored felt, then cut out all of the 2-inch by 2-inch squares.

Now create 18 of each shape in each color. Use the chart below to help you:

Shape	Red	Blue	Yellow	Green
♥	18	18	18	18
■	18	18	18	18
▲	18	18	18	18
▮	18	18	18	18

This will give you 16 of each shape in each color, plus 2 leftovers for each in case a piece gets lost. As mentioned earlier, you could use any shapes you want. I've chosen these because they are the easiest to cut out. To make the hearts, fold each piece in half, use white chalk to draw half a heart along the folded edge, then cut. Do the same for the triangles. For the squares, do nothing. For the rectangles, cut a square in half.

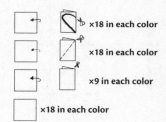

×18 in each color

×18 in each color

×9 in each color

×18 in each color

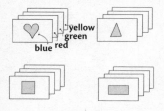

yellow
green
blue red

To make the sequence cards, draw each shape in each color on a separate card. For example, a red heart, a blue heart, a yellow heart, and a green heart, a red square, a blue square, a yellow square, and a green square.

Next, make 2 dice. Use the utility knife to cut out 2 pieces of foam board that follow the pattern shown. (Note: The picture shows dark grid lines, which will actually be very faint on the foam board.)

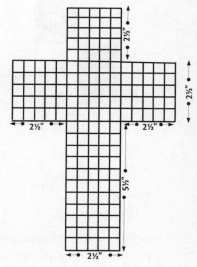

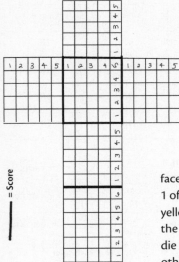

With the grid lines as a guide, use the utility knife and the edge of the ruler to gently score (cut halfway through) the foam board along the fold lines marked in the picture.

With the grid lines facing up, draw the faces of each die. On the first die, color each side 1 of the 4 colors you are using (red, blue, green, yellow). Mark the other 2 sides "Wild Card." On the other die, draw each shape on a face of the die (heart, square, circle, rectangle). Mark the other 2 sides "Wild Card."

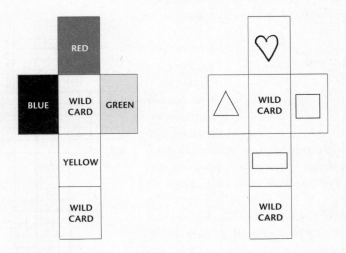

Now fold each die as shown, with the colors or shapes facing out. Secure each seam on the inside with transparent tape.

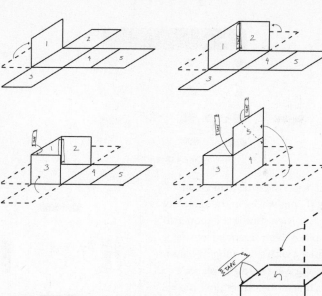

Once you fold the last side down, trim any excess that hangs over, then use transparent tape on the outside of the die.

▶ How to Play

Give each player a board and a set of 4 of each shape in each color. Use the chart to check that each player has all the correct pieces:

Shape	Red	Blue	Yellow	Green
♥	4	4	4	4
■	4	4	4	4
▲	4	4	4	4
▮	4	4	4	4

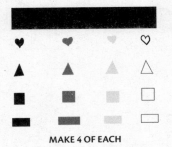

MAKE 4 OF EACH

Before you begin the round, agree on how many shapes will be in the sequence (4, 6, 8, or 10). Then shuffle the sequence cards and place them facedown in the center. Starting with the youngest player, each person draws a card and places it faceup in a line in the center until the number of shapes in your sequence is reached.

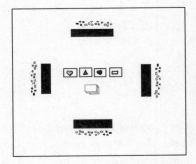

Now players take turns rolling the dice to determine what shape and color they can lay down to re-create the pattern in the center. For example, if you roll yellow and circle, you can put down only a yellow circle on your board and must put it in the correct place in the sequence. If you don't roll a combination that is in the sequence, you can't put anything on your board.

THE SEQUENCE

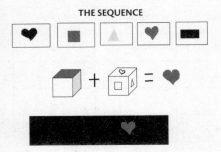

The first player to roll the correct combinations to re-create the sequence on his or her board wins!

QUILTING BEE

Players race to create pretty patchwork designs in this game.

■■■ **PLAYERS** 2 or more

MATERIALS (FOR 4 PLAYERS)
- foam board or heavy corrugated cardboard
- utility knife*
- 4 pieces black felt (12 inches by 12 inches)
- 2 pieces felt in at least 4 different colors (such as, pink, yellow, green, and white; 12 inches by 12 inches)
- scissors
- masking tape

*Utility knives are *very* sharp and should be handled only by adults.

▶ Prep Work

First, make the playing boards by cutting out one 9-inch by 9-inch square of foam board for each player. Center the board over the 12-inch by 12-inch piece of black felt.

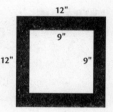

Snip off the corners of the felt. Pull 1 flap of felt up over the edge of the foam board and secure with tape. Next, tug on the opposite flap of fabric so the felt is taut, then fold that flap up and over the foam board and secure with tape. Do the same with the 2 remaining flaps of felt.

Next, measure and mark a 4-row by 4-column grid on the colored pieces of felt. Cut out the squares so that you end up with sixteen 3-inch squares in each color.

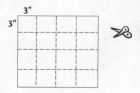

► How to Play

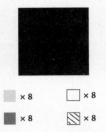

Give each player a board and 8 squares of each color.

 × 8   ☐ × 8

▨ × 8   ◩ × 8

Choose a leader for the round. The leader turns around and creates a pattern on the grid by laying down felt squares in a 3-by-3 quilt pattern (see the examples). Then the leader reveals the quilt to the other players, who race to match it on their grids.

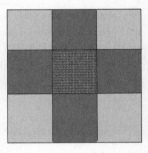

EXTRA FUN

◆ To make the game easier, start with a 3- or 4-block row rather than a grid.

◆ To make it more challenging, use a 16-square grid or cut half of the squares for each player in half to form triangles.

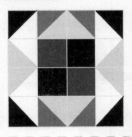

FUN FACT

The Amish, the group most known in the United States for their beautiful, intricate quilts, initially made plain single-color quilts in wool or cotton because anything more fancy was considered too worldly.

FOAM BOARD

BOY, DO I love me some foam board! It's durable, easy to cut, lightweight, and strong—perfect for making things at home! It's also easy to find. Most office supply stores will have some near the poster board.

FACTS ABOUT FOAM BOARD

- Foam board is made of polystyrene (a kind of plastic used to make things such as plastic forks, DVD cases, insulation, and disposable cups) sandwiched in between two long sheets of paperboard.
- Foam board was first made in 1957 by the Monsanto Company, which gave it the trade name Fome-Cor. It was mostly used by people in the graphic arts, but it's now used for displaying fine art and crafting.
- One advantage foam board has over heavy cardboard is that is resists warping so it's great for building things. It's also very light, which means you can pick up and carry that great thing you just built!
- However, because it's made from polystyrene, it decomposes over a long period of time and might give off acidic vapors, especially when it's exposed to UV light and air pollution.

How to Cut Foam Board

1. Foam board usually comes in different size sheets (such as twenty inches by thirty inches or thirty inches by forty inches). Some foam board will have faint one-inch grid lines on one side. Use these as guides when measuring and cutting.

2. To trim foam board to a size specified in a project, first use a yardstick and a marker to measure and mark straight lines to the dimensions needed.
3. Next, lay the yardstick along the straight line.
4. Run the utility knife along the edge of the yardstick (making sure your fingers are out of the way) to make a long clean cut through the foam and the paperboard.

CAR RACE

Here is a fun and easy theme-based board game for beginners.

■■■ **PLAYERS** 2 or more

MATERIALS
■ **foam board** ■ **utility knife*** ■ **ruler** ■ **masking tape**
■ **yardstick** ■ **markers (permanent ones, like Sharpie brand, work best)** ■ **1 tiny toy car for each player**

*Utility knives are *very* sharp and should be handled only by adults.

▶ **Prep Work**

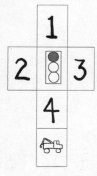

First, make the foam board die by following the directions from Sequence Sequence Super on page 110. On the faces of the die write 1, 2, 3, 4, a picture of a tow truck, and a picture of a red light.

Next make the game board by placing the 2 remaining pieces of foam board end to end so you have a long 20-inch by 60-inch piece. Run a line of masking tape across the seam where the boards join. (Do this only on the underside of the race track so you can fold the board in half when you're done.)

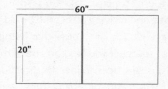

Flip the game board over and use a yardstick (or the guidelines if your foam board has them) and the markers to create four 5-inch-wide lanes. Next, measure and mark twenty 2-inch spaces in each lane. Mark the first space "Starting Line" and the last space "Finish Line."

Now, on each lane add some special spaces to spice up the drive from start to finish. Here are some ideas, but use your own imagination:

> 3rd space: "Repair Shop"
> 6th space: "Pot Hole: Lose a Turn"
> 10th space: "Flat Tire: Go to the Repair Shop"
> 12th space: "Fast Lane: Skip Ahead 2 Spaces"
> 16th space: "Speeding Ticket: Lose a Turn"

► How to Play

Give each person a tiny toy car as a playing piece. Starting with the youngest player, take turns rolling the die and moving across the board. If you get a 1, 2, 3, or 4, move that number of spaces. If you land on one of the special spaces, follow the directions there. If you roll a "tow truck" you can move any car to that player's Repair Shop space. If you roll a "red light" you lose a turn. First one to the finish wins the race!

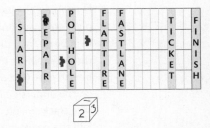

- Create more complicated tracks such as an oval or a figure-eight with more special spaces.
- Make up your own theme (such as a Fairy Race or Monster Race) and change the playing pieces, die, special spaces, and decorations to match.

FUN FACT

The Indianapolis Motor Speedway, which hosts the Indy 500 and the Brickyard 500 races, is the world's largest spectator sporting facility with more than 250,000 seats.

RING AND PEG GAME

Any home carnival needs this game in which contestants toss paper cup rings over drinking straw pegs.

PLAYERS 1 or more

MATERIALS
- 9 large paper cups
- yardstick
- scissors
- foam board
- marker
- utility knife*
- 5 pairs of disposable wooden chopsticks
- 9 drinking straws
- masking tape

*Utility knives are *very* sharp and should be handled only by adults.

▶ Prep Work

First, make the rings by cutting off the top 1 inch of each paper cup.

Next, use your utility knife on top of a safe cutting surface to trim your foam board into a 24-inch by 24-inch square. Use your yardstick and marker to make a dot in the center of the foam board. Make dots 12 inches to the left, to the right, above, and below the center dot. Finally, make dots 6 inches diagonally from the center in 4 directions. Now you will have a diamond shape with 9 dots.

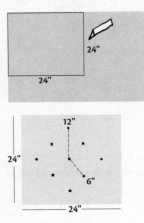

Pull the wooden chopsticks apart and trim each leg to 3 inches. Then trim the drinking straws to 3½ inches.

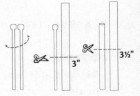

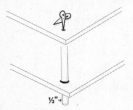

Gently and carefully, use one blade of the scissors to poke a small hole on each dot you drew. Work a straw through each hole. (Widen the holes with the tip of the scissors blade if necessary but don't make it too big because you want a snug fit for the straw.) Pull ½ inch of the straw through the bottom of the board.

Cut a slit on each side of the ½ inch of the straw sticking through the bottom of the board. Fold these 2 flaps down so they lay flat against the bottom of the foam board. Secure with a piece of masking tape. Repeat with the other 8 straws in the other 8 holes.

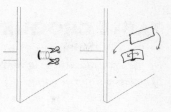

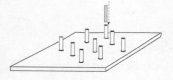

Set the board upright so the straws are standing up. Push the 3-inch chopsticks into each straw. Now you have 9 pegs.

Finally, use your marker to assign point values to each peg.

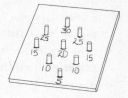

▶ How to Play

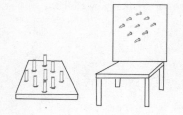

You can play this game 2 ways, either with the game board on the floor so the pegs stick upright or with the game board propped up on a table or chair so the pegs point forward.

Whichever way you face your board, make a masking tape line 3 to 5 feet away. Players take turns standing on the line and tossing the paper cup rings toward the pegs. Total up the points for any rings that land on the pegs. The player with the highest score wins!

TABLE CROQUET

No perfectly manicured lawn? No problem. Here is a simplified tabletop version of a classic summer game.

■■■ PLAYERS 1 or more

MATERIALS

- foam board ■ utility knife* ■ piece of felt (24 inches by 36 inches) ■ scissors ■ masking tape ■ yardstick or tape measure ■ drinking straw ■ disposable wooden chopstick ■ white chalk or pencil ■ 3 chenille stems (aka pipe cleaners) ■ large sewing needle or safety pin ■ hinged clothespin (1 per player) ■ marble (1 per player, each a different color)

*Utility knives are *very* sharp and should be handled only by adults.

▶ Prep Work

Use a utility knife on a safe cutting surface to trim your foam board to 20 inches by 30 inches. Then spread out the piece of felt on your work surface. Center the foam board sheet on top of the felt and trim the corners of the felt across the diagonal.

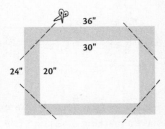

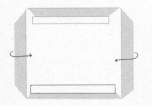

Fold one end of the felt around the bottom of the foam board and attach with masking tape. Then pull the opposite side of the felt very taut so that there are no wrinkles or bubbles on the other side and secure it with tape. Use the same method to secure the remaining 2 edges of felt to the foam board.

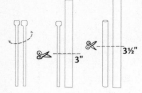

To make a peg in the center of the board, first trim the drinking straw to 3½ inches and the wooden chopstick to 3 inches.

Flip the foam board over so the felt side faces up. Find the exact center of the board, then gently and carefully use one blade of the scissors to poke a hole in the center spot.

Work the straw through the hole. (Widen the hole with the scissors blade if necessary but don't make it too big because you want a snug fit.) Pull ½ inch

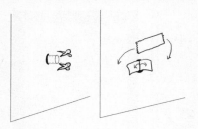

of the straw through the bottom of the board. Cut a slit down one side of the straw poking out of the bottom of the board and another on the opposite side. Fold these 2 flaps down so they lay flat on the bottom of the foam board and secure with a piece of masking tape.

Flip the board over so the felt side faces up. Push the 3-inch chopstick into the straw. Now you have the center peg.

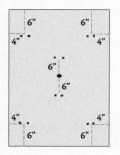

Next, you will measure and mark where 6 wickets will go. With the short side of the board facing you, measure down 6 inches from the center peg and use the chalk to make 2 dots, 2 inches apart, as shown. Repeat this on the other side of the peg. Then measure in 4 inches from the side and 6 inches from the bottom. Make 2 dots 2 inches apart. Do the same on the other side of the board. And again from the top.

To make the hoops, trim 6 chenille stems to 5 inches. Pluck a ½ inch of the fuzz from each end of each stem so that you leave the wire exposed.

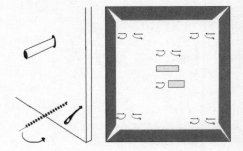

> **HELPFUL HINT**: This is easy to do. Chenille stems are made of thin wire twisted around fuzz. Pull out the fuzz using your fingers.

Next, use the large sewing needle to poke a hole through one of the white chalk dots. Make sure the needle goes all the way through the felt and the foam board. Work the wire end of a chenille stem through this hole. Do the same for the adjacent hole (poke it with the needle and work the other end of the chenille stem wire through). Flip the board over. Fold the wire down against the board and secure it with a piece of masking tape. Repeat for all the hoop markings.

Flip the board upright, and you will have six 2-inch-high chenille stem arches.

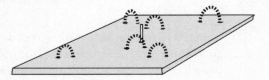

▶ How to Play

First, give each player a clothespin and a marble (each player should have a different color). To hit the marble, a player stands the clothespin upright with

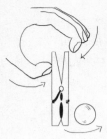

its jaw end on the felt. Hold the clothespin legs between thumb and forefinger. Place a marble in front of the clothespin. Squeeze the legs so that the clothespin opens and kicks the marble forward.

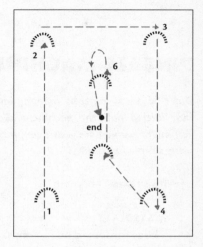

Players take turns hitting their marbles through the hoops in the correct order, as shown, and by sticking to the rules.

The real rules of croquet are quite complicated and involve cutthroat tactics such as "roqueting" another person's ball out of bounds and blocking wickets. For this version, the rules are stripped down to the following basics:

1. Each player gets 1 hit per turn.
2. Players may hit only their own marble with their own clothespin (in other words, players can't whack someone else's marble with their clothespin).
3. A wicket counts only if the ball goes through the arch in the correct direction and the correct order (as shown).
4. Players may knock other players' balls off course or out of bounds. As long as a marble is on the board, it is in play. If a marble goes off the board, the player may place it back on the board, 1 clothespin's length from the edge approximately where it went off.
5. If a player's marble hits another player's marble and knocks it through a wicket, that wicket will count for the other player as long as it was the next one to be completed by that player.
6. The first player to complete all the wickets in the correct order and hit the center peg is the winner.

PINBALL MACHINE

Don't be discouraged by the long materials list for this pinball game. It's not that hard to make the machine, and everyone will get into playing. Who knows, you might even create your own pinball wizards with this homemade machine using simple mechanics.

▪▪▪ **PLAYERS** 1 or more

MATERIALS

- large cardboard box
- masking tape
- yardstick
- markers
- utility knife*
- foam board**
- ruler
- wrapping paper tube
- pumper from a bottle such as lotion, soap, or shampoo
- scissors
- pencil
- pushpins
- rubber bands
- craft sticks
- hinged clothespins (6 or more)
- large paper clips (6 or more)
- bottle caps (from soda or beer)
- nail
- hammer
- plastic food container lid
- paints
- paintbrushes
- scrap piece of wood
- glue
- Ping-Pong ball

*Utility knives are *very* sharp and should be handled only by adults.

**You will want the foam board to lay snug inside the bottom of the cardboard box for this project. I found a box that was 24 inches by 30 inches across the bottom, so I bought a sheet of foam core that was 24 inches by 36 inches and trimmed it to size.

▶ Prep Work

First, prepare the box. Turn it upside down and secure all the bottom seams with masking tape.

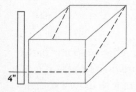

Flip the box over (so the bottom of the box is on the ground) and turn one of the short sides toward you. Use your yardstick to draw a straight line across the short side facing you that is 4 inches from the bottom of the box. Along the right side of the box, lay your yardstick diagonally from this line to the top right corner in the back and draw a line. Repeat for the left side.

4"

Now, using your yardstick as a straight-edge guide and your utility knife, cut along the left side diagonal line, across the front line (4 inches from the bottom), up the right side diagonal line, and along the back top seam. When you are done, your box should look like this.

Next, with the front of the box facing you, measure 4 inches in from each side and draw a vertical line. Use the utility knife to cut straight down along these lines to make a flap cut. Now your box should look like this.

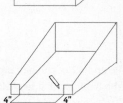

4"   4"

Lay the foam board on a large work space. Set the box on top of it so that 2 edges of the box line up with 2 edges of the foam board. Use a marker to trace the other 2 edges of the box on the board. Remove the box and, using a yardstick as your guide, cut along the inside edge of the lines with a utility knife so that the foam board will fit snugly inside the box.

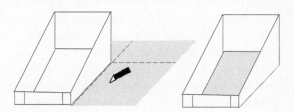

Now you will make the ball lanes and shooter. First, measure the long side of the box. Trim the wrapping paper tube to two-thirds this length. For example, if the long side of the box is 36 inches, cut the tube to 24 inches (36 inches × ⅔ = 24 inches).

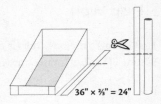

36" × ⅔" = 24"

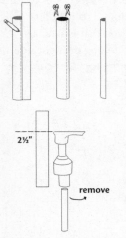

Now create 2 half pipes from the wrapping paper tube by standing the tube up on its end and holding the yardstick next to it to draw a straight line down the side. Do the same thing on the other side, directly opposite the first line. Cut along these lines to make 2 half pipes out of the tube.

2½"

remove

To make the shooter, remove the tube from the end of the pumper. Measure from the bottom of the large plastic piece to the top of the pumper. For example, mine is 2½ inches long.

Position 1 of the half pipes in the front right side of the box 2½ inches (or the length of your pumper) from the 4-inch wall. This will be the entry lane. Cut the other half pipe to

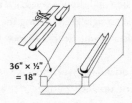

36" × ½" = 18"

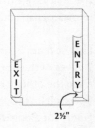

E X I T

E N T R Y

2½"

half the length of the box (so if the box is 36 inches long the second half pipe will be 18 inches long). Lay it down on the front left side of the box so it butts up against the 4-inch wall. This will be the exit lane.

Lay the pumper next to the entry lane (they should touch) so the bottom part of the tube touches the 4-inch wall. Lightly draw a circle around the tube then

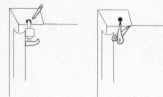

remove the pumper and use one blade of the scissors to gently and carefully bore a hole through this circle.

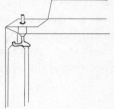

Slide the tube of the pumper through this hole (you want a snug fit) until the bottom of the bigger plastic piece touches the 4-inch wall and the spout of the pumper is directly below the lip of the half pipe.

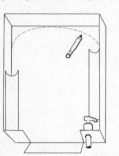

Next, use your pencil to mark an arch across the top of the foam board from the right top corner of the entry alley to the opposite side of the box.

Insert a pushpin into the foam board directly above the right top corner of the alley. Loop a rubber band over the pushpin. Take another pushpin and loop the other side of the rubber band around it. Pull the rubber band so that it is taut (but not stretched) then insert the pushpin along the penciled arch line. Continue doing this along the arch line from the right side of the box to the left.

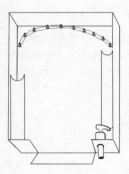

HELPFUL HINT: Don't stretch the rubber bands too much or the pushpins will ricochet out of the foam board—youch!

Next, you will make the flippers out of jumbo craft sticks inside the jaws of wooden hinged clothespins. First, place 2 clothespins with jaws facing each other horizontally 3 inches from the front edge of the box and 3 inches from the 4-inch walls on the left and right side. Make light marks with your pencil at each end of the clothespins so you can remember where they go. Next, lay a craft stick alongside each of the clothespins and adjust them until there is 1 inch between them. Mark each craft stick where the jaws meet at the hinge on the clothespins.

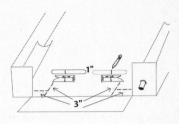

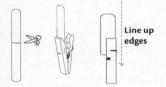

Line up edges

Cut the craft sticks where you made the marks. Pinch open the clothespins and slide in the craft sticks, cut edge first. Line up the edges of the clothespins with the edges of the craft sticks so they will lay flat.

Reposition the flippers by placing the clothespins on the pencil marks you made earlier. (Double-check to make sure there is 1 inch between the ends of the crafts sticks.)

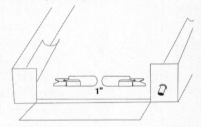

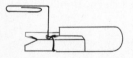

To attach the flippers to the foam, lift the outside arm of a large metal paper clip. Hold the clothespin steady with one hand while pushing the arm of the paper clip through the center hole of the clothespin hinge, through the foam board. Repeat for the other clothespin.

Remove the pumper then lift the foam board and insert the straight arm of a paper clip through the bottom of one of the holes so the arm sticks out of the top of the foam board

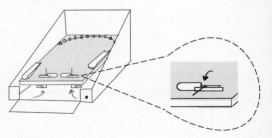

and the rest of the paper clip is snug against the bottom of the board. Then slip the clothespin over the paper clip arm. Repeat with the other paper clip and clothespin. Last, bend the paper clip arms down over the clothespins to hold them tight against the board.

Put the board back down and replace both ball alleys to the left and right of the flippers. With your pencil and yardstick, lightly draw a line straight across the foam board from the top of the exit alley on the left to the entry alley on the right. Now, lightly draw an arc from the top right corner of the exit alley on the left side of the box to the tip of the clothespin leg on the left side. Do the same on the other side, starting at the horizontal line you drew, down to the tip of the clothespin leg on the right side. As you did with the top barrier, place pushpins and rubber bands along these arcs.

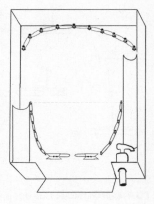

Now you have your basic pinball machine with a shooter, entry alley, exit alley, barriers, and flippers. Pretty cool, huh? Not cool enough for true pinball wizards! The real fun is in designing all the gewgaws for the balls to go through in the center. Here are some ideas:

SPINNERS: Make a small hole in the center of a metal bottle cap by laying the bottle cap upside down on a scrap piece of wood. Hammer a nail through the center. Remove the nail. Use a pushpin to attach the bottle

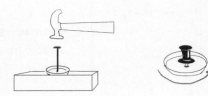

cap to the foam board. When the balls roll by, the caps will rattle and spin.

ALLEYS AND TUNNELS: Use masking tape loops and the leftover piece of your half pipe to make an alley on the board. Or use a paper towel or toilet paper tube to make a tunnel (just be sure your Ping-Pong ball can easily roll through the tube).

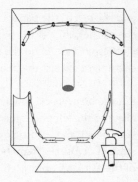

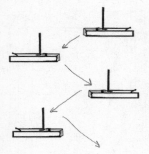

ZIGZAG: Attach clothespins in a zigzag pattern down one side of the board using large paper clips like you did for the flippers only leave the arms sticking straight up so that the clothespins can move freely as the ball cascades between them.

TURNAROUNDS: Cut out a half moon shape from one end of a small plastic lid (such as from a butter tub). Attach the lid to the foam board with a pushpin. The ball will enter the lid and turn around (or maybe get stuck until you turn it).

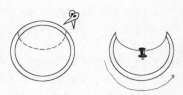

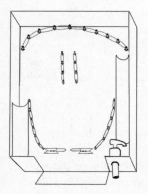

BOUNCY BARRIERS: Use more pushpins and rubber bands to make bouncy barriers in the center of the machine.

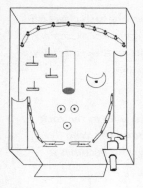

Once you've created your own design, go back and secure everything with a bit of glue. For example, use masking tape loops or glue to secure alleys and tunnels. Lift the board and put strips of masking tape over the bottom of the paper clips holding the flippers and zigzags to the board. Put some glue under the pumper. Put a little dab of glue under each pushpin. But don't put any glue or tape under the spinners or the turnarounds.

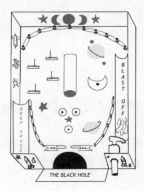

Finally, decorate! Use markers, poster paint, and/ or stickers to decorate the board and the box. For a more authentic pinball look, choose a theme (like a fairy castle, monster trucks, or outer space).

▶ How to Play

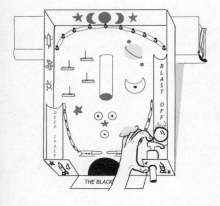

Prop the back end of the pinball machine up on 2 big books so it is at a slight angle. Line a ball up in the entry alley. Reach around the 4-inch wall on the right side and depress the pumper. Quickly let the pumper go to shoot the ball up the alley and into the center of the pinball machine. Use your index fingers to flip the flippers when the ball rolls toward you.

Keep the ball in play as long as you can. The ball is dead when it goes through the flippers and out of the box or when it gets stuck in the exit alley.

If you're looking for competitive pinball either see how long each player can keep the ball alive or assign point values to all the gewgaws. For example, 2 points for each spinner, 3 points for the zigzag, 5 points for the center alley, 6 points for a turnaround and −3 points if the ball gets stuck.

FUN FACT

The 1969 song "Pinball Wizard" was part of the rock opera Tommy *by the British rock band the Who about a deaf, dumb, and blind boy who becomes a pinball champ.*

PENNY PACHINKO

Here's a quiet game of chance for 1 or more players based on a Japanese arcade game called Pachinko.

▪▪▪ **PLAYERS** 1 or more

MATERIALS
- sturdy lid from a medium cardboard box* ▪ yardstick or ruler
- pencil ▪ foam board** ▪ utility knife*** ▪ 100 to 125 pushpins
- glue ▪ 22 small rubber bands ▪ 12 pennies

*For example, the lid from a box containing a ream of paper.

**If you can find the kind with a premarked ½-inch grid, snatch it up for this project.

***Utility knives are *very* sharp and should be handled only by adults.

▶ Prep Work

First, you will cut 2 pieces of foam board that will fit snugly inside the box lid. To do this, measure the length and width of your box lid (mine is 14 inches by 18 inches), then subtract ¼ inch from 2 sides (so my measurements are 13¾ inches by 17¾ inches). Measure and mark these dimensions on the foam board, then

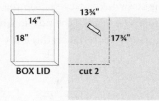

lay the board on a safe cutting surface. (I like to put a sturdy piece of corrugated cardboard underneath.) Use a yardstick or ruler as a guide and cut along the lines with a utility knife. Repeat for another piece of foam board.

Now you will draw a grid on 1 piece of foam board as a guide for where to put your pushpins. (Skip this step if your foam board already has a grid.) Orient the board so that the long sides are the top and bottom (like landscape mode for a computer document). Use your ruler and pencil to draw horizontal lines 1 inch apart across the width of the board.

Find the center point on the top and bottom lines you drew and make a mark on each (mine are at 9 inches because my box is 18 inches wide). Draw a vertical line to connect these 2 marks.

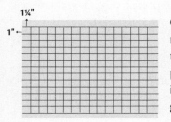

On the top and bottom lines, measure and mark 1¼ inches to the left and to the right of the center line and draw vertical lines at these points. Continue drawing vertical lines every 1¼ inches to the edge of the box. Now you have a grid made up of 1-inch by 1¼-inch boxes.

Put both pieces of foam board inside the box with the grid facing up. To create the slot where you will drop the pennies into the game, draw a line across the top inside edge of the box lid where it meets the foam board. Next, draw a rectangle centered on this line that is the same width as the center 2 squares

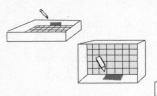

on your grid (about 2½ inches wide) and ½ inch tall. Turn the box lid up on its end (so the top edge is facing down) on a safe cutting surface and use a utility knife to cut out this slot from the inside of the box lid.

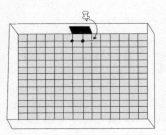

Now you will make a pushpin pyramid starting on the top row with 3 pins centered on the board. Place the first pin where the top horizontal line of your grid meets the center vertical line. Then place 1 pin at the intersection of the top horizontal line and vertical lines immediately to the left and right of the first pin.

Next you will place 4 pushpins on the second row so that they are to the left and right and smack dab in between the 3 pins on the top row.

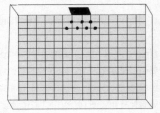

Continue like this on each row so that you add 1 additional pushpin each time (so that row 1 has 3 pushpins; row 2, 4 pushpins; row 3, 5 pushpins; etc.), staggering them so that no pin is directly below another pin from 1 row to the next.

HELPFUL HINT: If your box lid is narrower than mine, you may reach the edges. No problem. Just keep going the same way, staggering the pins each row from one edge to the other.

Stop when you get about 2 inches from the bottom of the box. (On my box, which is 14 inches, this equals 11 rows. But, as always, don't sweat the dimensions. If you have a narrower box lid, you will have fewer rows. If your box lid is wider, you'll have more rows.) Finally, place a row of pushpins along the bottom edge of the lid directly below the last row of pins.

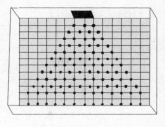

Once you have the all pushpins where you want them, lift the pins one at a time, put a dot of glue around the hole, then push the pin back down. Set aside to dry.

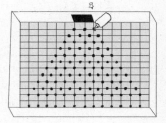

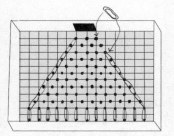

Now you will add the rubber band borders. Loop a small rubber band around the first and last pushpins in the top row and attach them diagonally to the first and last pins 2 rows down. Continue this way to the second-to-last row, then place a rubber band from each pushpin in the second-to-last row to the pin directly below it in the last row to create a series of alleys. (In mine, I created 11 alleys.)

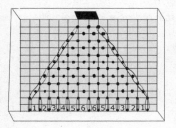

Finally, write point values in the alleys along the bottom edge of the lid.

► How to Play

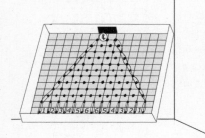

Lean the box lid against a wall so that it is at about a 30-degree angle (you know, enough so that the pennies will slide through the slot and bounce around the pushpins without popping out of the lid).

Lay a penny flat so it slides through the slot at the top, then watch as it bumps and bounces through the pushpin pyramid to an alley at the bottom. (Sometimes, pennies will get stuck on top of a pushpin. Gently—gently, I say—give the lid a little shake to dislodge the penny and send it on its merry way.) Do this for all 12 pennies then add up the point total.

The player with the most points wins.

Real Pachinko is a crazy-popular Japanese game that's a cross between a slot machine and a pinball machine. Players sit mindlessly in front of their blinking, bonking, banging machines, shooting silver balls into a peg pyramid and watching them fall into slots at the bottom. Certain combinations of slots win prizes (like tickets for more balls!). Like most good games, Pachinko started as a kids' game just for fun.

HULA HOOPS

THEY WERE ALL the craze in the 1950s, but like every classic toy, they've prevailed and are still popular today. But you can do more than twirl them around your hips as this set of games will prove.

FACTS ABOUT HULA HOOPS

- Hoops are ancient toys and have been made from metal, bamboo, wood, and other plants. Ancient Egyptian children probably made them from dried grape vines. The ancient Greeks may have used them to exercise.
- The Brits gave hoops to their kids to play with in the 1300s.
- The *hula* part of the name comes from the hula dance, in which dancers sway their bodies in smooth gliding motions to tell a story.
- In 1948, Richard Knerr and Arthur "Spud" Melin started the toy company Wham-O, which manufactured slingshots and Frisbees and eventually plastic hula hoops. They considered calling them swinga-hoops and twirl-a-hoops, but settled on hula hoops instead.
- Today, in addition to being fun toys, hoops are used by grown-ups for cardiovascular exercise and toning.

GIANT RING TOSS

What if giants had summer birthday parties? They'd play giant ring toss in the yard!

PLAYERS 1 or more

MATERIALS
- 6 or more 1- to 2-foot-long sticks
- large grassy area
- 1 hula hoop

▶ Prep Work

Push sticks into the ground in a big open circle with each stick about 2 feet apart. Push the sticks far enough into the ground so that they are upright and sturdy. Choose 1 stick to be "home" then assign point values to the other 4 sticks as shown:

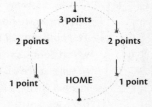

▶ How to Play

First player stands behind the home stick and flings the hula hoop toward any other stick, trying to ring it. If the hula hoop makes it around a stick, the player gets those points.

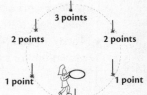

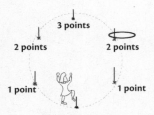

Each player gets to toss the hoop 5 times. Then total up the points to see who wins.

EXTRA FUN

◆ To make the game more interesting, create a course by pushing sticks into the ground along a path. Players take turns tossing the hoop to each stick in order. See who can ring the most sticks along the course.

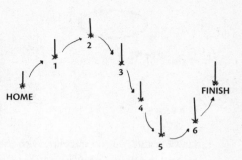

HUMAN HOOP RELAY

Teams advance down the field by alternately hooping one another.

■■■ **PLAYERS** 4 or more in groups of 2

MATERIALS

■ lightweight hula hoops (1 hoop for each pair of players)

▶ **Prep Work**

None.

▶ **How to Play**

Find a big open playing field and determine the start line and finish line (from the tree to the driveway, for example). Divide the players into teams of 2 and give each team a hula hoop.

The object is for each team to get their hoop from the start line to the finish line, with this catch: The only way to move your hoop forward is to toss it over your partner (like a giant human ring toss game), following these rules:

1. Player A stays on the start line with the hoop while player B moves toward the finish line. Player A tells player B when to stop. When player B stops, player A tosses the hoop and tries to ring B.

2. If the hoop rings B, then B stays put and player A moves toward the finish line. Player B tells A to stop, then player B tries to toss the ring around player A.

3. If the ring misses, then the player who threw it must stay put while the other player retrieves the hoop and returns to where the first player is standing. Then the player can move forward again until the thrower says stop.

4. Continue this way (alternating who moves forward and who tosses) until 1 team reaches the finish line.

PREDATOR AND PREY

The laws of the wild come into play as one animal group evades another in this tag and chase game.

■■■ **PLAYERS** 4 or more (but lots of players is lots more fun)

MATERIALS
■ index cards (4 per player) ■ markers ■ 4 to 8 hula hoops
(depending on the size of the group)

▶ **Prep Work**

First, change the name of this game to whatever diametrically opposed animal duo your group likes (you could be cats and mice, lions and zebras, or jewel wasps and cockroaches if you want).

Next, use markers to decorate 4 index cards per player with the food source of the prey animal. For example, for mice draw cheese, for zebras draw grass, for cockroaches draw old melon rinds, stinky cheese bits, and discarded crusts of bread.

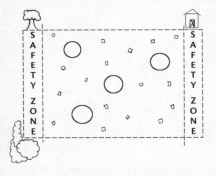

Determine the boundaries of your playing field such as the entire backyard or the oak tree to the baseball diamond. Identify a safe zone at either end of the field (such as past the tree, in the driveway). Then lay the hula hoops around the playing field between the safe zones. For a small group, use only 4 hoops, but for large groups, use up to 8 hoops. Next, scatter the food cards all around the playing field.

▶ How to Play

Use your favorite "You Are Not It" game to figure out who will be the predator (cat, lion, jewel wasp, or whatever you've decided on). The other players will be the prey (mice, zebras, cockroaches, etc.). Half the prey animals line up at one end of the field inside the safe zone

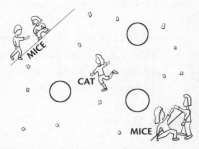

and the other half line up on the opposite side safe zone. The predator stands in the center of the field.

Prey animals run back and forth from one safe zone to the other to gather 4 food cards, 1 at a time, without being tagged by the predator while following these rules:

1. Prey animals can pick up only 1 food card per trip across the field (from one safe zone to the other).

2. Prey animals must gather 4 food items and wind up in a safe zone without being tagged to survive.

3. Prey animals may collect no more than 4 food cards (that is, no hoarding food so other animals starve!).

4. Hula hoops are hidey holes. The predator cannot tag prey animals who are inside a hula hoop hidey hole. However, prey animals may stay in a hidey hole for only 5 seconds at a time.

5. Prey animals cannot hide inside the same hula hoop 2 times in a row. In other words, prey animals must move to a different hula hoop after 5 seconds. They can go back to a hoop they've been in before, but only if they've been in a different one first.

6. If a predator tags a prey animal, the prey animal must scatter any collected food cards on the ground again.

7. Once a prey animal is tagged by the predator, you can pretend that the prey animal is dead and must sit out on the sidelines until the game is over. Or, if you're into weird sci-fi twists to normal ecology, the prey animal can become a predator and help tag other prey animals.

Once all the prey animals are either safe or dead, the game is over.

EXTRA FUN

- Play the global warming version (wait . . . did I say *fun*?) in which there's not enough food for all the animals by making only 2 food cards per player but keep the rule that each prey animal has to collect 4 cards to survive.

- For large groups start with 2, 3, or 4 predators and make everybody else a prey animal.

AROUND THE HOOP

A fun party game for large groups who'll get tangled up with giggles.

■■■ PLAYERS 8 or more players

MATERIALS
- hula hoop

▶ **Prep Work**

None! Get going already.

▶ **How to Play**

Divide players into 2 equal teams and arrange each team in a circle.

Place a hula hoop over 1 person's arm then ask each group to join hands.

Teams race to move the hoop all the way around the circle without breaking the chain of hands.

HOOP JOUSTING

When you think of jousting, you may envision men in armor falling noisily off horses, but jousting tournaments had lots of games other than poking each other.

■■■ PLAYERS 3 players

MATERIALS
■ 2 brooms ■ open grassy area ■ 1 hula hoop

▶ Prep Work

None.

▶ How to Play

The 3 players stand in a triangle about 10 feet apart from each other. Two players stand across from one another, each straddling a broom as if it were a horse (you know with the bristly side toward the back). The third person holds the hoop.

The person with the hoop rolls it between the other 2 players, trying to keep it straight down the middle. The other 2 players gallop forward and try to catch the hoop with the broom handle, without falling off their "horse."

Keep score as follows: The jouster who catches the hoop gets a point. If no one catches the hoop, the roller gets a point. Play 5 rounds. The player with the most points wins and gets to choose which position to play in the next round, or kiss the hand of the queen who's watching from her fancy tent.

FUN FACT

In true jousting, two armored knights battled with lances (long, heavy, pointed spears) while on horseback. This mock battle, which could be deadly, was popular entertainment for the rich and royal during the Middle Ages.

OLD BLIND FOX TOSS

Man alive, Mr. Fox is having problems today. He's blind and he lost his tail. No worries, though, you can still have fun in this goofy game of catch.

■■■ **PLAYERS** 5 or more

MATERIALS
■ panty hose ■ scissors ■ tennis ball ■ blindfold ■ hula hoop

▶ Prep Work

To make the foxtail, use scissors to cut 1 leg off the pantyhose (or use a single nylon stocking) and drop the tennis ball into the toe. Tie a knot just above the ball.

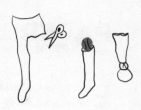

▶ How to Play

In this game, every player will have a turn to be the blind fox, so first, determine the order of players. For example, go youngest to oldest or do a quick round of your favorite "You Are Not It" game to determine which player will go when.

6 ft

Blindfold the first fox and give him or her the tail. All the other players hold the hula hoop as a group. Position the fox about 6 feet away from the hula hoop group.

Players must follow these rules:

- ◆ The fox must spin around 5 times to get good and dizzy before throwing the tail.
- ◆ The fox must throw the tail higher than his or her own head.
- ◆ The hula hoop group must move as a unit, with everyone holding on to the hoop with at least one hand, while trying to catch the tail.
- ◆ The hula hoop group may begin moving as soon as the fox starts spinning.

If the group misses the tail, the fox scores a point and gets to throw his tail again. If the group is able to get the tail to land inside the hoop, then it's the next player's turn to be the fox.

Once every player has had a turn to be the fox, the fox with the most points wins!

PAPER

EVERYDAY ORDINARY PAPER, huh? What's so fun about that? Lots! You can fold it, write on it, and draw on it with endless variations so the fun might never stop.

FACTS ABOUT PAPER

- The invention of paper is credited to Ts'ai Lun, a Chinese scholar who registered his invention with the emperor of China in AD 105.
- Paper was originally made by soaking plant fibers (such as wood, hemp, or grass, and later linen or cotton rags) in water until they broke down into what was called the pulp. The pulp was then poured over fine-mesh sieves (like a screen) so the water ran off, leaving only the fibers, which were dried. This thin layer of intertwined fibers made paper.
- Most paper today is made in large mills or factories, but the process remains the same. Companies use large machines to turn wood fiber (which consists of tiny cellulose strands held together by lignin, a natural glue) into pulp, then they spray the pulp onto a conveyor belt of fine-mesh screens, then dry it.
- More and more, companies are adding recycled paper to their pulp. About 80 percent of the paper you put in your recycling bin can be used again. The other 20 percent is trash such as wires, staples, paper clips, plastic, or fibers that have become too weak to use again. Paper can be recycled only five to seven times before the fibers are too weak to be used again.
- When paper is recycled, the ink, glue, and weak fibers are removed during the pulp process. That mix is then separated

from the water (which the factory can use again). The stuff that's leftover can be burned to make energy, composted, put in a landfill, or be used to make concrete and gravel.

◆ So remember to always use both sides of your paper, then put it in the recycling bin when you're finished!

SQUIGGLES

This will surely become a favorite quiet, noncompetitive game for 2.

■ ■ ■ **PLAYERS** 2 players

MATERIALS
- paper ■ **2 different colored pens or pencils**

▶ Prep Work

None.

▶ How to Play

The first player draws a squiggle on the paper.

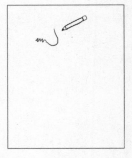

The second player uses a different colored pen or pencil to create a picture out of the squiggle.

Then switch and play again until your paper is full.

- For kids just learning to write their ABCs, play the Squiggles Alphabet Version. Player 1 draws an *A*. Player 2 makes a picture out of the *A*. Then player 2 draws a *B*. Player 1 makes a picture out of the *B*. Continue this way until you reach the end of the alphabet.

FUN FACT

The cave drawings in Lascaux, France, are more than 17,000 years old and depict horses, deer, bulls, and hunters.

HOW MANY WORDS?

An old birthday party favorite, good for a quiet moment with a group.

■■■ **PLAYERS** Any number

MATERIALS

■ 1 piece of paper per player   ■ 1 pencil or pen per player   ■ clock or stopwatch

▶ **Prep Work**

None.

▶ **How to Play**

Write a name, word, or phrase on the top of the page. For example, at a birthday party, write the full name of the birthday person (*Heather Anne Swain*), or a holiday phrase (*Happy Halloween*).

HEATHER ANNE SWAIN

Players race for 5 minutes to write as many words of 3 letters or more as they can by rearranging the letters and using only the letters that appear in the original word or phrase. In other words, if there is only one *E* in the original word or phrase, then each new word can have only one *E*.

When time is up, compare lists to see who has the most number of unique words. In order to do this, the first player reads the words on her list. The other players cross off any of these words on their lists. Then the next player reads words left on his list and other players cross off the words they have in common. Continue this way until all the players have read their words. Then players count the number of unique words left on their list. The player with the most words wins.

NAME THAT ANIMAL

Make animal masks and then play 20 questions to guess the critter.

■■■ **PLAYERS** 2 or more

MATERIALS

■ paper ■ pencil ■ 10 flimsy 8-inch paper plates ■ scissors
■ markers or crayons ■ 10 jumbo craft sticks ■ masking tape

▶ Prep Work

Make a list of 10 (or more) animals. For example:

1. cow
2. dog
3. cat
4. pig
5. parrot
6. zebra
7. lion
8. eagle
9. fly
10. mouse

Next, make a paper plate mask for each animal. First, hold a plate up to your face (or a friend's) and with a pencil *gently* sketch around the eye area.

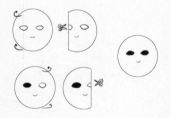

With the plate away from your face, find the center of one eye. Fold the plate lengthwise at this point and trim around the eye. Do the same for the other eye. Hold the mask up to your face to make sure the eye holes are in the right place. Use this plate as a template for the other 9. Lay it on top of the next plate, trace around the eye holes, then cut the eyes out. Repeat for all plates.

Now, use markers or crayons to draw an animal's face on each plate.

Flip the plates over and attach a craft stick to the bottom using masking tape to make a handle.

► How to Play

Mix up the masks and place them facedown in a pile. Players take turns picking up a mask by the handle and looking through the eye holes without looking at the front. Then the player asks yes-or-no questions about themselves. For example:

Q: Am I a mammal?
A: Yes.
Q: Do I live in the wild?
A: No.
Q: Do I live with people?
A: Yes.
Q: Do I live on a farm?
A: Yes.

Continue until the player guesses the animal.

Q: Am I a cow?
A: Yes!

EXTRA FUN

◆ For younger children who have trouble following the logic of yes-and-no questions, the other players can offer clues about the animal until the child guesses correctly.

RUTABAGA

Do extras in movie scenes really say rutabaga *over and over again to make background chatter? I don't know, you'll have to ask an extra. But whether it's true or not, it sure sounds funny in this word-substitution game.*

■■■ **PLAYERS** 2 or more

MATERIALS
- 10 (or more) index cards
- pen or pencil

▶ Prep Work

Write and/or draw a picture of one action word (aka verb) on each card. For example, *run*, *sneeze*, *jump*, and *sleep*.

▶ How to Play

Shuffle the cards and place them facedown in a pile. The first player draws a card without showing it to anyone. Now, the player starts talking, replacing the action word with the word *rutabaga* while the players try to guess the action. Players should follow these rules:

1. When it is your turn, you may not say the action word on the card or use any motions to show what it is.
2. Instead, you must replace the action word with the word *rutabaga* while you're talking.
3. If you say the action word or use motions, you lose your turn and have to sit down.

For example, if my word is *run*, I might say, "When I *rutabaga* too hard, I get a cramp in my side. Kids like to *rutabaga* on the playground because they have a lot of energy after sitting in the classroom all morning. Some people like to *rutabaga* races like marathons or sprints." The first person to guess the word gets to draw the next card and rutabaga the word.

FUN FACT

A rutabaga is a cross between a turnip and a member of the cabbage family and probably turned up in Europe in the 1600s in gardens where turnips and cabbages grew side by side, fell in love, and started a little rutabaga family.

DOT-TO-DOT GRID

This is one of those classic rainy-day, pencil-and-paper games that fosters logic and strategy skills that are good for other games such as checkers and chess.

■■■ **PLAYERS** 2

MATERIALS
■ piece of paper (graph paper is great for this, but not necessary; 8½ inches by 11 inches) ■ pens or pencils (different colors are good)

▶ Prep Work

Draw a 10 by 10 grid of dots on the paper.

▶ How to Play

Players take turns connecting 2 adjacent dots (either across or up and down, but not diagonally) on the grid.

> **HELPFUL HINT**: Having each player use a different color pen or pencil is nice because you can clearly see each other's moves.

Continue taking turns until someone connects 2 dots that complete a square. That person puts his initial inside the square and then goes again until he can no longer make any squares.

> **HELPFUL HINT**: As the game progresses, long runs of squares develop. Setting up these runs is the fun part!

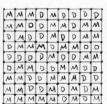

WINNER!
M = 43

D = 38

Continue like this, taking turns and making squares with initials inside, until the entire grid is filled with boxes and initials. Then each player counts up his or her initials. The player with the most initials on the grid wins.

- ◆ To simplify the game, make a smaller grid (5 by 5). To make it more challenging, make a larger grid (20 by 20)

PIN THE *X* ON THE *Y*

Add your own spin to the classic Pin the Tail on the Donkey.

■■■ PLAYERS Any number

MATERIALS
- poster board ■ markers ■ construction paper ■ scissors
- tape ■ blindfold

► Prep Work

Determine the theme for your game, for example, Pin the Kiss on the Frog (princess party), Pin the Petals on the Flower (garden party), Pin the Leg on the Octopus (sea creature party).

Next, determine the *X* and the *Y* in which *X* is what will be pinned on *Y*. (Okay, that's a complicated way of saying *X* is the tail and *Y* is the donkey.) In our example, the game will be Pin the Kiss on the Frog.

Now draw a big frog (the *Y*) on the poster board. Next, make puckered lips for kisses (the *X*'s) for each player out of construction paper. On the front, write each player's name and on the back, place a small tape loop.

► How to Play

Surely, you've played Pin the Tail on the Donkey before, so you know the drill. Hang the poster of the frog on a wall at the players' shoulder height. Hand each player a kiss. Blindfold players one at a time, spin them around 3 times,

point them in the right direction and give them a gentle push. Watch them stumble toward the frog and attach the kiss in a funny place (like a kiss on the frog's tush!).

The player who gets the kiss closest to the appropriate place on the frog wins.

FUN FACT

Donkeys are part of the equine family, which includes horses, zebras, and mules (a cross between a horse and a donkey). Sometimes donkeys are born without tails, a genetic defect, which might be how the game Pin the Tail on the Donkey originated.

FARMERS' MARKET

Here's a good cooperative getting-to-know-you game for groups.

■■■ **PLAYERS** 4 or more

MATERIALS FOR 6 PLAYERS
- paper - pencil - 36 index cards - markers or crayons

▶ Prep Work

Count the players, then make a list of that number of fruits and vegetables that you would find at a farmers' market. For example, for 6 players, the list might look like this:

1. apple
2. grapes
3. kumquats (yes, there are kumquat farms!)
4. zucchini
5. curly kale
6. parsnip

Next, each player creates one complete set of fruit and veggie cards by drawing a picture of each farmers' market item and writing its name on an index card. In our game, each player would make an apple card, a grape card, a kumquat card, a zucchini card, a curly kale card, and a parsnip card. (Of course, 1 person could do all this prep work ahead of time, but it might be more fun to let all the players do it.)

▶ How to Play

Shuffle all the cards together, then pass out 6 cards to each player. Players must attempt to get a full set of cards by following these rules:

1. Each player may only have 6 cards at a time, no more and no less.
2. Players can exchange only 1 card with another person and then must move on to a different player.
3. Players can come back to each other but only after speaking to a different player first.
4. When a player has collected 1 of every item at the market (that is, 1 of each of the 6 cards) he or she may sit down.

5. If there are only 2 players left, those players can exchange as many cards as necessary.

While collecting cards, players walk around the room chatting with each other as if they were at a real market. They might sound a little something like this:

Player 1: Hello, do you happen to have any curly kale today?

Player 2: Why yes, I do. It's lovely sautéed with a little garlic.

Player 1: Thank you kindly. Anything I could get for you?

Player 2: Why yes, I could sure use a parsnip!

Player 1: Who couldn't? Parsnips are out of this world. But I don't have any today.

Player 2: How about a kumquat?

Player 1: Why, yes. Here you are.

Continue until every person has a full set, or 1 of each card, and has sat down.

EXTRA FUN

- Switch it up for a competitive challenge and tell players to collect only 1 item of their choosing. For example, try to get all the apples. One rule: You may not refuse to give up a card you have if another player requests it. The first player to get all 6 cards of his or her chosen item wins.

TREASURE HUNT

Stash a bag of that leftover Halloween candy somewhere in the house and follow one of these plans for creating a treasure hunt.

■■■ **PLAYERS** 1 or more

*Matches are dangerous and should be handled only by adults.

▶ Prep Work

Stow your treasure in a box or bag. If you want to get super-crafty, decorate the box or bag.

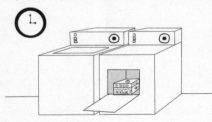

Now find a really good hiding place for the treasure (try under the azalea bush, behind the couch in the den, or inside the dryer).

Next, determine a starting point and a series of 5 or more clue locations that will lead the pirates to the treasure. It's best if you make the locations somewhat far apart so that the search is interesting. Here's one example:

Starting point: Front door

Location 1: Inside the right-side medicine cabinet door in the upstairs bathroom

Location 2: Behind the ficus tree in the dining room

Location 3: Under the duvet in the guest bedroom

Location 4: On top of the toaster oven in the kitchen

Location 5: Under the third couch cushion in the living room

Treasure hiding place: Inside the dryer in the basement

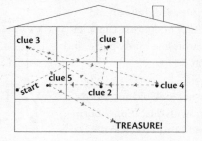

Now you'll make a series of clues. Each one will lead the pirates from one location to the next, where they will find another clue, until they get to the treasure. The clues should be as follows:

Clue 1: From starting point to clue location 1

Clue 2: From clue location 1 to clue location 2

Clue 3: From clue location 2 to clue location 3

Clue 4: From clue location 3 to clue location 4

Clue 5: From clue location 4 to clue location 5

Clue 6: From clue location 5 to the treasure hiding place

Your clues could come in many forms. For example, to get the pirates from the front door (starting point) to clue 1 (medicine cabinet) you could do any of the following:

Simple: Your next clue is under the toothpaste.

Involved: From the portal to the street, take 10 steps into the cave. Cross the threshold and turn left. Find the hill of 16 steps. Climb to the top. Slip through the third door on the left. Lower the white lid to cover the well. Step up. Open the small door in the wall on the right.

Riddle: Pirates of old have teeth full of mold from eating their hardtack and mush. Don't let yours go to waste, find this fine minty paste, and always be sure to brush.

For more fun, make the clues look old and worn. Wrinkle them, cover them with dust (flour), burn the edges of the paper, and/or rub them in dirt.

Now hide the clues as follows:

Clue 1: Keep because you will give this to the pirates to start the game

Clue 2: Hide in location 1   **Clue 3:** Hide in location 2

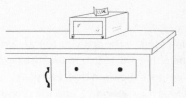

Clue 4: Hide in location 3

Clue 5: Hide in location 4

Clue 6: Hide in location 5

▶ How to Play

Gather up the scurvy dogs at the starting point. Explain you have found a series of old clues up in the attic in your great-great-great-grandmother's diary. Remember her? She was the one who was rumored to be known as Swashbuckling Sadie and sailed with Blackbeard before she settled down, had kids, and learned to make blackberry jam, right? Go on. Ham it up! The object of this game is for the group to locate the treasure, so they'll have to find a way to work together. Then give the pirates the first clue.

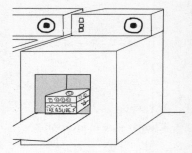

Pirates follow the first clue to location 1 where they will search to find the next clue. Once they find that, everyone follows it to location 2, and so on until they arrive at the treasure.

EXTRA FUN

◆ Try letting the players create treasure hunts for each other. Give each player a bag of treasure to hide and paper to write down clues, then they can take turns solving each other's mysteries.

FUN FACT

Did pirates really make maps to find their hidden treasure? Well, maybe. But most likely they divided the loot once they stole it.

PAPER CUPS

BEHOLD THE PAPER cup! We toss out a lot of these puppies without ever giving them a second thought, but they are quite marvelous when you start messing around with them because they're versatile and fairly sturdy. Consider playing a few of these games before you clean up after your next party.

FACTS ABOUT PAPER CUPS

- A man named Lawrence Luellen is credited with the idea for disposable cups in 1907 (first made of paper and later plastic) as a way to get a clean drink of water without having to share a dipper from a communal water barrel.
- The paper for paper cups arrives at the cup factory on large flat rolls. One side is covered in plastic or wax to keep the cup from falling apart once liquid goes inside. The other side can be printed with a design or color. Then the sheets are cut into "flats" which are rolled into cylinders and sealed by a machine. Next, the circles on the bottom of the cup are added and sealed. Finally, another machine folds the top edge down to form the rim.
- The artist Chris Jordan made a large scale photographic depiction of 410,000 paper cups stacked in columns to represent the number of disposable hot beverage cups thrown away every fifteen minutes in the United States. In real life these columns would be forty-two stories high and many blocks wide.

BUILD A TOWER

Take turns stacking cups higher and higher, but watch out—that Leaning Tower of Cupsa could topple at any moment!

PLAYERS 2 or more

MATERIALS

- ruler
- pencil
- corrugated cardboard or foam board
- utility knife*
- masking tape
- 1 pack large plastic or paper cups
- 1 pack medium plastic or paper cups
- 1 pack small plastic or paper cups

*Utility knives are *very* sharp and should be handled only by adults.

▶ Prep Work

On a safe cutting surface, use a utility knife to make a 1-foot by 1-foot square of cardboard. Then, cover the edges with masking tape to avoid sharp corners.

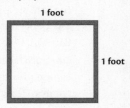

Give each player 5 large, 5 medium, and 5 small cups.

▶ How to Play

Players take turns placing 1 cup at a time on the playing board. Cups may face any way the the player

YES

NO

wishes (face up, face down, on their sides . . . which doesn't seem like a good idea to me, but what do I know?), *except* nesting inside one another. When the board is full, the only way to go is up!

Continue the game by stacking cups. For a cooperative game, see how high the group can make the tower. If everyone uses all the cups, keep going by taking cups off one at a time without knocking over the tower. If you want a little competition, then the person who knocks the tower over is out. Start again with the remaining players. Play elimination rounds until 1 player remains. Name that player King or Queen Cup!

FUN FACT *One of the most famous towers in the world is the Leaning Tower of Pisa in Italy. It is 187.27 feet tall on the high side and 186.02 feet tall on the low side and leans about 4 degrees to the left.*

KNOCK DOWN THE TOWER

This is an old carnival favorite made with a pyramid of cups and a beanbag to toss.

■■■ **PLAYERS** 1 or more

MATERIALS
■ **6 to 15 large paper or plastic cups** ■ **3 beanbags (see page 19 for directions on how to make your own)**

▶ Prep Work

Build a pyramid of cups on top of a table. For a
small setup, start with 3 cups on the bottom. For
a large setup, start with 5 cups on the bottom.

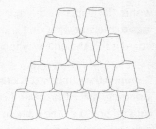

▶ How to Play

Players stand at the edge of the table and take 3 to 5 giant steps backward.
(Older kids take more steps back, younger kids take fewer steps) to determine
the starting line.

Try to knock down the tower by tossing the beanbags, 1 at a time, toward the table.
Score a point for each cup that falls down. Play 3 rounds and total up the score.

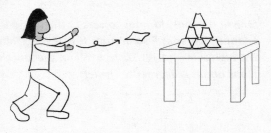

FUN FACT

*The world's largest paper cup just might be the
sixty-eight-foot-tall cup located in Riverside,
California, outside the former Lily-Tulip paper cup
factory . . . but really it's made of concrete and only
looks like paper.*

CUP BALL

A Native American classic made with modern items—a paper towel tube, string, aluminum foil, and a paper cup. Put them all together and see how many times you can get the ball into the cup.

MATERIALS

- **large disposable paper cup (9 ounces or bigger)** ▪ **paper towel tube** ▪ **pencil** ▪ **utility knife*** ▪ **yardstick or ruler** ▪ **masking tape** ▪ **string** ▪ **scissors** ▪ **aluminum foil**

*Utility knives are *very* sharp and should be handled only by adults.

▶ Prep Work

Place the cup upside down on a table and hold the paper towel tube centered on top of it. Trace around the tube with your pencil. Take the tube off and draw a cross in the center of the circle. Use the utility knife to carefully cut along the lines. Next, gently press the paper towel tube through the slits you just made so that it emerges 2 inches inside the cup with 4 flaps from the bottom of the cup surrounding it.

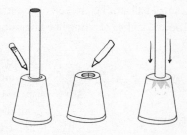

> **HELPFUL HINT**: Work carefully and slowly so you don't tear the bottom of the cup.

Remove the tube and tear off four 4-inch pieces of masking tape. Reach inside the cup and attach each piece of tape to a flap. Then push the tube back

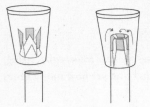

through the bottom of the cup and gently press the tape against the edges of the tube, fold it over the top of the tube and press it to the inside to secure. Set this aside.

Cut about 2 yards of string.

HELPFUL HINT: For a quick measurement, a yard is about the length from the tip of an average grown-up's nose to the tip of her pointer finger.

3 feet

Tear off a strip of aluminum foil and wrap it in a small ball around the top of the string, leaving about 6 inches of string hanging out of the top.

6"

2 yards

2"

Continue wrapping strips of aluminum foil around the first ball until you have a ball about 2 inches across with a few inches of string hanging out of the top. Tie a knot in the top of the string and trim the excess.

Tie the other end of the string around the paper towel tube just below the cup. Secure the string to the tube with a strip of tape.

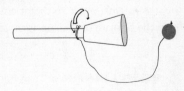

▶ How to Play

Hold the bottom of the paper towel tube and swing the ball, then try to catch it inside the cup. Challenge a friend and see how many times you can each catch it in a row.

HELPFUL HINT: For smaller children, wrap the string around the tube a few extra times to shorten it so the ball won't drag on the floor when swung.

MINI-MARSHMALLOW POPPER CONTEST

Make marshmallow poppers, then have a contest to see whose marshmallow goes the farthest . . . without being eaten.

PLAYERS 2 or more

MATERIALS TO MAKE 1 POPPER
- paper cup
- utility knife*
- scissors
- balloon
- rubber band
- mini-marshmallows

*Utility knives are *very* sharp and should be handled only by adults.

▶ Prep Work

Use a utility knife to cut the bottom out of the cup so you have a big hole.

Without blowing up the balloon, tie a knot in the end, then snip off the top ½ inch.

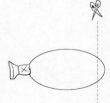

Stretch the balloon over the bottom of the cup so that the knot is in the center of the hole, then secure it with a rubber band around the cup.

► How to Play

In a large open space, determine a starting line. Players line up and insert their mini marshmallows into the opening of their cups, gently shaking the cup until the marshmallow snuggles down in the center of the balloon.

Players take turns standing on the line and firing their marshmallows by pulling the knot back and letting go. (Warning, do not shoot the marshmallow toward any person, no matter how much he or she begs you to.)

Once the marshmallow lands, the player finds it and stands in the spot where it landed. The person whose marshmallow goes the farthest wins.

EXTRA FUN

♦ Marshmallow poppers are a great way to use your measurement and graphing skills . . . and what could be more fun than graphing? For this project, you'll need:

- ○ paper and pencil
- ○ poster board
- ○ markers
- ○ long tape measure

♦ After each player shoots a marshmallow, use the tape measure to determine how far it went. Record each person's name and distance on a piece of paper. When everyone has shot a marshmallow, make a bar graph to show the results on the poster board.

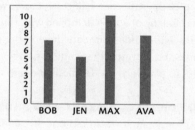

DIGITAL CAMERA AND PHOTO PRINTER

LONG, LONG AGO old-fashioned people like you used something called film inside cameras to take pictures. Then you had to travel long distances (like all the way to the mall or drugstore) to deliver this film to a person with a special machine the size of a small bus to process the film into photographs, which you had to schlep all the way back to the mall to pick up. And then half the pictures were out of focus or somebody was blinking or your hair looked weird and you had to throw out the pictures. No wonder someone invented a digital cameras the size of a brownie and a printer that could sit on your home desk! Here are a few games to play with this fabulous modern technology.

FACTS ABOUT DIGITAL CAMERAS AND PHOTO PRINTERS

- The idea for a camera is an old one. In 300 BC, the Greek philosopher Aristotle built a camera obscura (a dark box with a single small hole in one side to allow light to come in) to accurately capture a view of the sun.
- Around the year 1000, the Arabian scientist Ibn al-Haytham did a series of experiments with a room-size camera obscura and made the discovery that light travels into the eye. Before that, people believed the eye sent out rays to scan objects (neat idea for a superhero, but not true).
- Although people had a basic understanding of how the eye worked and how to capture images in the camera obscura, it wasn't until the invention of a chemical process called daguerreotyping that photography was possible in 1839.
- Digital cameras take advantage of technology that turns data (such as images and sound) into ones and zeros (called

bits) and stores them on a device (a teeny tiny chip) that can be read by a computer.

- Most photo printers use ink jets which spray itty-bitty dots (smaller than the width of a human hair) of colored ink precisely onto photo paper to reproduce the digital image.
- The next generations of photo printers are small enough to fit into your pocket. They connect directly to your camera and don't use ink jets! Instead, they use a special kind of paper that appears white, but really contains dye crystals that when heated by the printer turn different colors.

PICTURE CLUE SCAVENGER HUNT

Here's a twenty-first-century twist on an old favorite that uses visual cues for an around-the-house hunt.

■■■ **PLAYERS** 1 or more

MATERIALS
  ■ camera   ■ photo printer   ■ photo paper   ■ bag for each team

► Prep Work

Snap 10 pictures per team of child-safe, easy-to-reach objects around the house. For example, a pair of red socks inside someone's drawer, a green block from the toy chest, a rectangular plastic storage container from the kitchen drawer, and a can of pinto beans from the cupboard. Then print the pictures.

► How to Play

Divide the players into teams. Give each team a bag and 10 pictures. Then turn them loose to gather the booty from around the house. The first team to collect all the items on their pictures wins!

FUN FACT

In the 1979 movie Scavenger Hunt, *a millionaire game maker makes his relatives participate in a giant scavenger hunt to see who will inherit his fortune.*

PROGRESSIVE PHOTO SCAVENGER HUNT

You'll love this twist on a scavenger hunt using weird pictures of ordinary places around the house. The directions may sound complicated, but it's harder to explain than it is to do, and the payoff is super fun! We've played this at every birthday party my kids have had since they were three, and it never disappoints.

■■■ **PLAYERS** 2 or more

MATERIALS

■ camera ■ photo printer ■ photo paper ■ envelopes ■ small bag of treasure (such as coins, candy, or small toys)

▶ **Prep Work**

First, determine a route with 10 stops that you want the players to follow through the house. Here's an example:

1. Bathtub
2. Washing machine
3. Kitchen table
4. Behind bedroom lamp
5. Living room couch
6. Dining room hutch
7. Easy chair in the den
8. Linen closet
9. Kitchen cupboard
10. Behind the deck chair

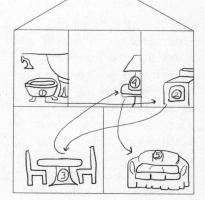

Next, take a photo of each place on the route.

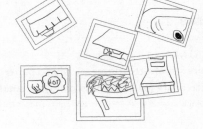

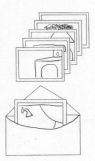

Print the photos and put them in order of the route, then put the first photo clue in an envelope (the photo of the bathtub in this example).

Now comes the tricky part. Hide the rest of the photos in progressive order so each one shows the next place on the route. For example, when players get to the bathtub, they will find a photo of the washing machine. When they get to the washing machine, they will find a photo of the kitchen table. At the kitchen table they'll find a picture of the bedroom lamp and so on.

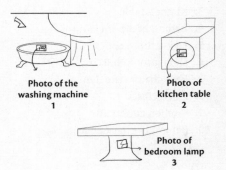

Photo of the
washing machine
1

Photo of
kitchen table
2

Photo of
bedroom lamp
3

At the last place on the route hide the treasure. For example, on my route, the treasure would be behind the deck chair.

► How to Play

Tell the players they will work as a group to find photo clues that will lead them to a prize. Give them the envelope with the first clue and watch them go!

EXTRA FUN

- ◆ If you have more than 5 players, make it a race by creating 2 different routes through your house (make sure they don't overlap). Divide the players into 2 teams and give each one an envelope with their starting clue. Let them race to see who finds the treasure first, but make sure there is enough treasure for everyone to share!

FRIENDS AND FAMILY MEMORY GAME

Remember that old favorite Concentration? Here's a twist using photos of the people in your life

■■■ **PLAYERS** 1 or more

MATERIALS
- ■ pictures of friends and family members (4 inches by 6 inches)
- ■ index cards or poster board (4 inches by 6 inches)   ■ glue

► Prep Work

Select and print pictures of family members and
friends so that each photo belongs to a pair and
you end up with 5 to 10 pairs. There are lots
of ways to do this. For example, make couples.
Grandma goes with Grandpa, Uncle Teddy goes
with Auntie Ginny, Neighbor Kay goes with her
kitty Flash. Or choose 2 different pictures of the

**Grandpa &
Grandma**

**Aunt Ginny
& Uncle Ted**

Kay & Flash

same people, for example Grandma in a bikini and Grandma skiing. Uncle Jerry
on a tractor and Uncle Jerry at a wedding. Another idea, match baby pictures to
current photos for each person or parents with one of their children.

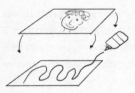

Glue each photo onto an index card. (Make sure all
the index cards are the same color.)

► How to Play

First, go through the cards with the players so everyone
recognizes and agrees on the pairs. Then shuffle the
cards and lay them out in a grid like you would for
Concentration or Memory played with regular cards.

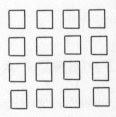

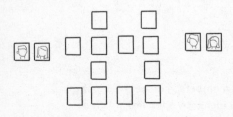

Take turns turning over 2 cards to try
to make a pair. If a player gets a match,
she takes the pair and can go again.
If the player doesn't get a match, she
turns both cards back over in their
original place and the next player
goes. The player with the most pairs at
the end of the game wins.

EXTRA FUN

◆ Who needs fancy-schmancy photo technology when you can draw pictures? If you don't have enough photos, let all the players draw family members and friends on index cards and play this game with original artwork.

FUN FACT

In 1958, Concentration became a TV game show that lasted for 3,796 episodes.

FRIENDS AND FAMILY GO FISH

Use the cards from the Friends and Family Memory Game (page 185) to play Go Fish.

PLAYERS 2 to 4

MATERIALS
- pictures of family members or friends (4 inches by 6 inches)
- index cards or poster board (4 inches by 6 inches) ▪ glue

▶ Prep Work

Follow the instructions for the Friends and Family Memory game on page 185 so you have at least 8 pairs of photos. Glue the photos onto the index cards.

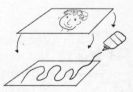

▶ How to Play

First, go through the cards with the players so everyone recognizes and agrees on the pairs. Then deal cards face down so that each player has 4 cards. Put 1 card faceup in the center of the players and the rest of the cards facedown in a stack. Collect as many pairs as possible following these rules:

1. The youngest player goes first and asks any other player if he or she has a particular card (for example, "Jenny, do you have Grandma Gigi?").
2. If Jenny has the card, she must hand it over. If she does not have the card she says, "Go fish!"
3. The player must choose 1 card from the pile in the center and discard 1 of his own cards faceup so that he has only 4 cards in his hand.
4. When the draw pile is empty, shuffle the discard pile and turn the cards over to become the new draw pile.
5. Any time a player makes a match, he puts those 2 cards down on the table.

When there are no more cards in the discard or draw piles, the player with the most pairs wins.

FUN FACT

The playing cards we're used to seeing have four suits (hearts, clubs, diamonds, and spades), but different cultures have different suits on their cards: in Germany, the suits are hearts, leaves, bells, and acorns, and in Spain, they are coins, cups, swords, and clubs.

PING-PONG BALLS

PERKY LITTLE PING-PONG balls are good for so many things besides table tennis. And they're easy to find in the toy aisle at a drugstore or the dollar store. So grab a pack today and amuse yourself with these games.

FACTS ABOUT PING-PONG BALLS

- Ping-Pong balls are made of celluloid, a tough flammable plastic made by combining cellulose (from the cell walls of plants), nitric acid, and camphor (a tough gummy substance from the camphor tree).
- To make the balls, sheets of celluloid are softened in hot isopropyl alcohol then pressed into a hemispherical (half of a ball) mold. Each half of the ball is made separately, then joined together with glue at the seam.
- Ping-Pong, or table tennis (its official name), was also known as wiff-waff when it was first played in Britain in the 1880s. Players used their dining room tables with books or cigar box lids as racquets and a golf ball or champagne cork for a ball.
- Although people have been playing table tennis (aka Ping-Pong) since the 1800s, it didn't become an Olympic sport until 1988 during the games in Seoul, South Korea.
- Did you accidentally step on your Ping-Pong ball? As long as you didn't put a hole it in, you can fix it. Here's how: Fill a coffee mug halfway with water. Heat the mug of water in the microwave for one minute (use a hot pad to remove it because the handle will be hot). Place the crushed ball in the mug then use an empty soda bottle (with a lid on) to push and hold the ball under the water. Hold for thirty to sixty seconds and your ball should reshape itself!

BALL TO$$

In this game, teams compete to see who can get the farthest apart and still catch the ball.

■■■ **PLAYERS** 2 of more

> **MATERIALS**
> ■ 1 large paper or plastic cup (9 ounces or bigger) per player
> ■ 1 Ping-Pong ball per pair of players

► Prep Work

None.

► How to Play

Give each player a cup then divide players into pairs and give each pair a Ping-Pong ball.

Pairs of players start standing toe to toe with the ball in one player's cup. Pass the ball from 1 cup to the other. Each time a team successfully gets the ball from 1 cup to the other without dropping it, both players take 1 step back so they are moving away from one another.

As players get farther apart they will have to toss the ball and catch it. See which duo can get the farthest apart without dropping the ball.

FUN FACT

In jai alai (pronounced hi li*), players throw and catch a very hard rubber ball (called a pelota) with specially curved wicker baskets (called cestas). It is one of the world's fastest sports with balls traveling up to 180 miles per hour.*

BUCKET TOSS

My best childhood friend, Heidi, and I played this game endlessly on the sidewalk in front of her house. Most of the fun was from taking turns commentating for each other.

■■■ **PLAYERS** 1 or more

MATERIALS
■ 5 sticky notes (such as Post-it brand) or 5 small pieces of paper and transparent tape ■ marker ■ 5 nonbreakable containers (such as sand buckets, large yogurt containers, or food storage bowls) ■ masking tape ■ 5 Ping-Pong balls

▶ Prep Work

Write the numbers 10, 20, 30, 40, and 50 on the self-adhesive notes and attach one to each container.

Lay down a line of masking tape on the floor to be the starting line. Line up the buckets in consecutive order 1 foot from the starting line and then each bucket 1 foot from the next.

▶ How to Play

Players take turns standing with their toes on the starting line and tossing the Ping-Pong balls into the containers in order (first in the 10-point bucket, next in the 20-point bucket, etc. up to the 50-point bucket).

Add up the points for each bucket with a ball in it. The player with the most points wins the Grand Prize! (Oh right, you'll need a Grand Prize . . . maybe a brand new car or a refrigerator? I'll let you work that one out.)

> **FUN FACT**
>
> *This game is based on the Grand Prize Game from The Bozo Show, a TV program out of Chicago in the 1960s hosted by a red-haired clown named Bozo. The grand prize for tossing balls into six buckets on the show was a new bicycle and money!*

MICRO GOLF

For the miniature golf fans in your life, create a roll-up felt course with a nifty shooter made from a clothespin and paper clip.

■■■ **PLAYERS** 1 or more

*Felt sold by the yard usually comes in either 36- or 72-inch widths. For this project, I used 36-inch-wide felt.

► Prep Work

To make the course, cut out 9 fairways from the dark green felt that are 4 inches wide and between 18 and 30 inches long. Your fairways should be different lengths and different shapes (some straight, some curved to the left, some curved to the right, maybe one with an S-curve shape).

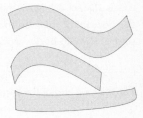

To make a hole, place an empty toilet paper tube at one end of a fairway and trace around it with white chalk. (This happens to be the perfect diameter for a Ping-Pong ball.) Then fold the felt in half along the circle, snip it with the scissors, open the felt back up, and trim out the circle. Repeat for all the fairways.

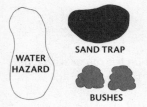

Now create some hazards. Cut out a few differently shaped water hazards from the blue felt. Make some sand trap shapes from the beige felt. Create bushes and trees from the dark green.

Finally, cut out nine 1-inch squares of red felt. Number these 1–9 with the permanent markers.

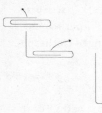

To make a golf club, pull the outside arm of a paper clip straight until the clip is shaped like an *L* and there is 1 loop remaining.

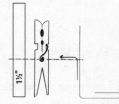

Next, measure from the bottom of a clothespin leg to the center of the hole in its hinge. (On my clothespins this is 1½ inches). Now, measure that distance from the bottom of the *L* on the paper clip. Bend the top part of the clip backward at this point.

Put the long end of the paper clip (the one you bent backward) through the hole in the hinge of the clothespin. Stand the clothespin up on its legs and the paper clip will become the head of the golf club. Repeat to make a club for each player.

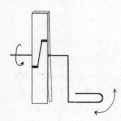

To swing the club, hold the clothespin steady with one hand and twirl the paper clip with the other.

▶ How to Play

First, design your course. Spread out the 2-yard piece of light green felt on a large flat surface. Choose any number of fairways and arrange them on the course. Mark their order with the red numbered squares. Add the hazards.

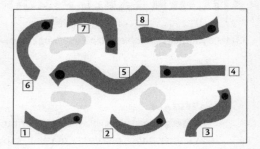

Players take turns positioning their golf clubs and Ping-Pong balls at the top of each fairway. Spin the club head to whack the ball down the fairway. Count how many strokes it takes to get the ball to stop in the hole. Add a stroke if the ball goes into a hazard. The winner is the player with the fewest strokes.

When you're done, the winner gets to design the next course!

FUN FACT

It's hard to know when golf became a game because people have been hitting balls with sticks into holes for as long as there have been holes, sticks, and balls. However, the game we now play probably originated in Scotland in the fifteenth century. Miniature golf (or Putt-Putt, a well-known franchise), on the other hand, has a clearer history. It started as miniature replicas of real golf courses and developed into family fun with obstacles like windmills and bridges.

KITCHEN TABLE PING-PONG

Change your kitchen table into a Ping-Pong court with a homemade net and paddles.

■■■ **PLAYERS** 2 or 4

MATERIALS

■ 4 toilet paper tubes ■ yardstick or tape measure ■ 4 6-inch heavy-duty paper plates ■ masking tape ■ scissors ■ scraps of corrugated cardboard or foam board ■ rectangular kitchen or dining room table ■ 2 C-clamps* ■ 3-inch-wide elastic bandage** ■ self-adhesive hook and loop fastener tape (aka Velcro) ■ 1 Ping-Pong ball

---

*C-clamps come in different sizes. The 2-inch clamps work well for my table, but if you have a really thick table, you might need bigger clamps.

**If you use large C-clamps, choose a larger bandage, such as 4 or 5 inches wide.

▶ Prep Work

To make the paddles, lay a toilet paper tube on the back of a paper plate so 3 inches of the tube are below the edge of the plate. Put a long strip of masking tape halfway into the tube with the rest attached to the back of the plate. Then place long strips of tape across the tube and onto the plate. Repeat for the other 4 racquets.

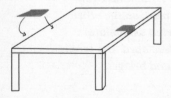

To make the net, cut out two 4-inch by 8-inch strips of cardboard or foam board. Find the center of the long side of your rectangular table and wrap 1 of the strips around the edge of the table to protect the surface.

Attach a C-clamp over each piece of cardboard.

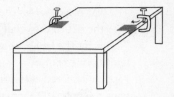

Unroll the elastic bandage. Cut 3-inch strips of the self-adhesive hook and loop fastener tape.

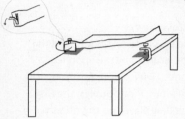

Attach the corresponding pieces together, and remove one side of the adhesive backing and press the sticky side to the end of the elastic bandage. Fold the bandage around the C-clamp and pull taut. Remove the adhesive backing from the other side of the hook and loop tape and press the elastic bandage against it.

Stretch the bandage across the table and fold it around the other C-clamp. If necessary, trim the bandage so that the end will wrap around the C-clamp and meet the rest of the bandage at the front of the clamp. Then attach the self-adhesive hook and loop fasteners as you did for the other side.

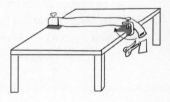

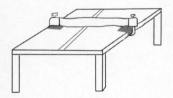

If you're planning on playing doubles (that's with 4 players at once) and it's okay with the owner of the table, run a line of masking tape down the center of the table from one end to the other.

▶ How to Play

For singles, 2 people play one another. For doubles, teams of 2 play each other. Players can abide by the official rules of table tennis or just have fun pinging the ball back and forth, but here are the basics:

1. The first player serves the ball by bouncing it on the table and hitting it over the net to the other side.
2. Players hit the ball back and forth (this is called a rally). Players may either let it bounce or not.
3. A point is scored every time the ball is in play (not just when the server wins the point). Opponents gain a point in the following cases:
    a. the server fails to get the ball across the net
    b. a player misses the ball
    c. a player fails to get the ball across the net
    d. a player hits the ball too hard so that it doesn't bounce on the other side of the table and is not returned by the opponent
    e. a player allows the ball to bounce twice before returning it
4. Each player serves for 2 points, then switches. (For doubles, the first player on the first team serves, then the first player on the other team, then switch back to the second player on the first team, then the second player on the second team.)
5. The first player to reach 11 points wins; however, the game must be won by at least 2 points. In other words, matches may continue past 11 points until a player has 2 more points than the other.

Now grab your paddles and Ping-Pong balls for a kitchen table battle.

FUN FACT *World class Ping-Pong players can hit the ball up to one hundred miles per hour!*

PLASTIC SODA BOTTLES

DON'T TOSS ALL of those leftover soda bottles into the recycling. First, check out this collection of games from bowling to bombardment.

FACTS ABOUT PLASTIC SODA BOTTLES

- Before plastic bottles were invented, most beverages were packaged in glass.
- In 1917, Webster Byron Baker invented a plastic bottle cap so that caps could be fit to the bottles, instead of bottles being fit to caps.
- Although plastic food and drink containers (like Tupperware) became popular in the 1940s, plastic wasn't used to package soda until much later.
- Nathaniel Wyeth patented the process for making plastic bottles in 1973.
- Most soda bottles are made from polyethylene terephthalate (PET), which is soft when heated then blown into bottle-shaped molds and left to cool.
- The good news about plastic bottles is that they are lightweight and don't shatter. The bad news about them is that plastic is probably not stable and some of the chemicals may be leaching into our drinks.
- Although PET plastic can be recycled, every time plastic is melted down to reuse, the quality degrades, meaning new plastic must be added to the mix. For that reason, most recycled PET bottles are "down-cycled" into products such as plastic lumber and polar fleece.

ROLLING PIN BOWLING

Here's a simple and fun way to keep things rolling on a rainy day.

PLAYERS 1 or more

> **MATERIALS**
> masking tape ▪ a long, smooth floor ▪ yardstick ▪ 10 1-liter plastic bottles (empty, clean, and dry) ▪ rolling pin

▶ Prep Work

First, make a 2-foot-wide by 5-foot-long alley with masking tape on the floor.

Set up the bottles in a triangle arrangement with the first bottle centered behind one end of the alley. Place the rolling pin on the line at the opposite end of the alley.

► How to Play

Take turns rolling the pin from one end of the alley to the other, knocking over as many bottles as possible.

Score 1 point for each bottle knocked over on each roll. Except for when the player knocks over all the bottles on one roll (a strike) which is worth 15 points! The player with the highest score after 10 rolls wins.

FUN FACT

Real bowling is usually played with ten pins and a large, heavy ball that has three to five finger holes. On each turn, players get to roll the ball two times in a row to see how many pins they knock down. If they knock down all the pins on the first roll that's a strike and they get ten points plus two more rolls. If they knock all the pins down after two rolls that's a spare and they get ten points plus one more roll.

RING AROUND THE BOTTLE

Here's the home version of the carnival game, only this one isn't rigged so you just might win.

▓▓▓ **PLAYERS** 1 or more

MATERIALS
- 5 large paper cups ▪ scissors ▪ funnel ▪ 5 cups of uncooked rice ▪ measuring cup ▪ 5 empty half-liter soda bottles with lids ▪ yardstick ▪ masking tape

▶ Prep Work

First, make the rings by cutting off the top 1 inch of 5 paper cups.

HELPFUL HINT: Gently squeeze the cup to flatten it a bit to make the first cut. Then, work one blade of the scissors inside the cup and leave one blade on the outside of the cup so you can cut around in a circle.

Use the funnel to pour 1 cup of rice into each bottle. (If you don't have a funnel, roll a piece of paper into a cone and put the small end into the bottle.) Then screw the lid on tightly.

Line up the bottles 6 inches apart on a table.

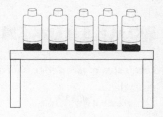

▶ How to Play

Lay down a line of tape 5 feet from the table to make the starting line. Players take turns standing on the line, tossing the rings toward the bottles. The player who can get the most lids around the bottles wins.

Are carnival games really rigged so you can't win? Probably not. The games are just hard enough to master so that most players won't win prizes, and even if they do, the prizes are so cheap when bought in bulk that the carnival still makes money as long as enough people pay to play the games.

BOMBARDMENT

This is sort of like dodge ball, only you don't get beaned in the head . . . maybe.

■■■ **PLAYERS** 2 to 6

MATERIALS
■ chalk or a jump rope (to mark the center line) ■ 20 empty plastic bottles (various sizes are good) ■ 2 rubber playground balls

► Prep Work

In a big open space determine the boundaries of your playing field, which should be at least 10 feet by 10 feet, but the field can be any size that makes sense for the number of players and the area available to you. Mark a center line on the field with chalk if you're on concrete or a jump rope if you're on grass.

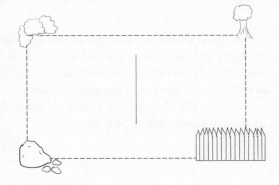

► How to Play

Divide the players into 2 teams. Give each team 10 empty bottles to set at the far end of their side of the playing field. They can do this any way they want as long as

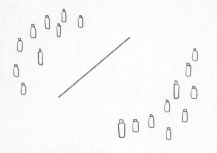

the bottles are within the boundaries of the field. Part of the fun of this game is developing strategies for how to set up the bottles.

Players scatter across their own sides of the field but may never cross the center line. Give each team a ball. When the game begins, 1 player from each team throws the ball toward the opposite side's pins to knock them down. Players on the opposing side try to catch or block the ball without crossing the center line. When a ball goes out of bounds, a player must retrieve it. If a bottle gets knocked over (either by a ball or by a player's clumsy feet) it cannot be set up again. The first team to have all its pins knocked over loses.

BOTTLE ALLEY

Have a recycling bin full of empty soda cans and bottles? Here's a fun way to use them before trash day.

■■■ **PLAYERS** 1 or more

MATERIALS
■ sidewalk or driveway ■ chalk ■ many empty plastic bottles and/or aluminum cans ■ broom ■ ball (such as a rubber playground ball)

▶ Prep Work

With chalk, draw a curvy course that is 3 feet wide along the driveway or sidewalk, then line the edges with empty bottles and cans.

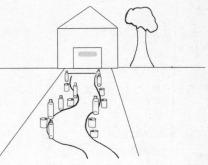

▶ How to Play

Take turns guiding a ball through the course with a broom without knocking over the bottles or cans. Time each player as he goes through the course, then add 1 second for every bottle that falls over. The player with the lowest time wins.

FUN FACT

This game is based on curling, an Olympic sport in which teams take turns sliding large smooth stones across an ice lane toward a target while a sweeper brushes the ice to help the stone move closer to the target.

GUARD THE BOTTLE

Here's a good, active game to get your ya-yas out.

■■■ **PLAYERS** 4 or more

MATERIALS
- 1 hula hoop per player*   ■ 1 empty plastic bottle per player
- rubber playground balls (1 less than the number of players, so if there are 5 players, you will need 4 balls)

*No hula hoops? No problem! If you're playing on concrete, use chalk to draw circles.

▶ Prep Work

Place the hula hoops in a large circle, then put an empty plastic bottle in the center of each hoop for each player.

▶ How to Play

Do rock, paper, scissors or draw straws to see which player won't get a ball at the start of the game. Then give each of the other players a ball.

As with soccer, this is a no-hands game, meaning you can kick the ball, you can stop the ball with your legs and feet, you can bonk it with your head, but you cannot touch the ball with your hands or arms.

Each player is assigned a hoop and must guard the bottle inside it. At the start of the game, players stand in front of their hoops and begin kicking their balls, trying to knock over the other players' bottles. Any time players don't have a ball, they should be guarding their own bottles or trying to retrieve loose balls to kick at their opponents. Anyone can go anywhere to retrieve a ball, but should beware of leaving his or her bottle unguarded for too long!

When a bottle gets knocked over, the player is out. Last bottle standing is the winner.

TINY TOYS

YOU'VE PROBABLY GOT close to a million little dudes hanging around your house. They come from gumball machines and birthday party gift bags and sometimes, I'm convinced, they procreate in the toy boxes at night. Here are several fun ways to put those guys to good use.

FACTS ABOUT TINY TOYS

- Imagine a world with no toy stores, catalogs, or online shopping. What on earth would children do? Turns out they did just fine making toys out of whatever they could find lying around. Rags became dolls. Pig bladders became balloons. Sticks and rubber bands become slingshots.
- But eventually some mighty smart people in the early 1800s figured out that they could make and sell toys to kids pretty cheaply, and the toy business began.
- Early manufactured toys were made out of wood, tin, or cast iron, then later rubber got in the game. Today plastic is the big winner in toy manufacturing.
- One of the earliest U.S. toy companies was Mattel, which began in 1945. They first made picture frames, then dollhouses, but eventually they made nothing but toys like Barbie and Hot Wheels.

WHAT'S MISSING?

Get out your tea tray for a sweet old-timey kids' game that the Brits used to play.

▪▪▪ **PLAYERS** 1 or more

MATERIALS
- tray ▪ 10 to 20 small toys and/or items from around the house

► Prep Work

None.

► How to Play

Arrange the little toys (for example, a Lego piece, wooden block, bouncy ball, finger puppet, and plastic fish) on the tray. For younger players, use fewer objects, for older players, use more. Let all the players study it for 1 minute.

Then turn around and remove 1 object; don't let the other players see which one is removed. Let the players see the tray again.

The first player to guess correctly what's missing gets to arrange the objects for the next round.

STUFFED ANIMAL CHARADES

Here's a fun and easy introduction to charades using your favorite cuddly soft friends.

■■■ **PLAYERS** 2 or more

MATERIALS
- ■ pillowcase ■ 10 different small- to medium-size stuffed animals

▶ Prep Work

Put all the stuffed animals in the pillowcase.

► How to Play

One player takes the pillowcase
out of sight of the other players
and pulls out an animal.

The player returns and acts out
the animal for the others to guess.
Unlike in grown-up charades,
sounds are okay in this game but
talking is not. The first person to
guess the animal correctly chooses
the next animal to act out.

FUN FACT

*Charades probably started in France in the sixteenth
century with a popular parlor game called* petit
jeux *in which people made up riddles as clues to
guessing a word or phrase. Later, acted charades
became popular in Britain and the United States, in
which teams take turns acting out words or phrases
one syllable at a time.*

PILOLO

Here is a traditional Ghanian game that combines an obstacle course with a scavenger hunt.

■■■ **PLAYERS** 1 or more

MATERIALS
■ **4 toys** ■ **stopwatch**

▶ Prep Work

Set up an obstacle course route through the house, then walk the players through it. For example, start at the back door, run zigzag through a maze of kitchen chairs, hop over a yardstick, circle the dining room table, crawl under the piano bench, ride the skateboard to the living room, roll across the couch, hop on 1 foot down the front hall, and touch the doorknob.

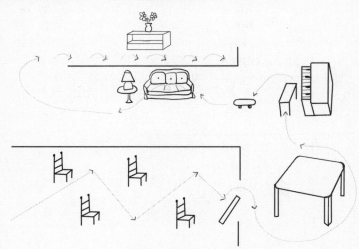

Next, show all the players the 4 toys, then ask them to close their eyes while you place the toys in strategic hiding places along the course. For example, a stuffed dog is under one of the kitchen chairs, a dump truck is beside the piano, a plastic mermaid is behind a lamp, and a robot is on the shelf in the front hall.

► **How to Play**

Use the stopwatch to time each player as he or she runs the course and gathers the toys along the way. After each player goes, rehide the toys again along the path. Mix up the hiding places so players who go later don't have an unfair advantage. If someone misses a part of the course, he or she must go back and do it correctly. The person who finds all the hidden toys and correctly completes the course in the shortest amount of time wins.

POPCORN

Make your own parachute out of an old sheet and then give your favorite soft friends a bouncy ride.

■■■ **PLAYERS** 4 to 8

MATERIALS
■ queen- or king-size flat sheet ■ marker ■ scissors ■ 1 small stuffed animal per player

▶ **Prep Work**

Fold the sheet in half, then half again the other way.

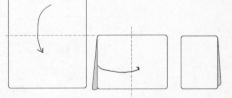

On the closed corner of the folded sheet, draw an arc about 2½ inches from the edge. Then cut along the arc to remove the corner. Open the sheet and you will find a 5-inch circle cut out of its center.

► How to Play

Spread the sheet out on the floor and have each player hold a corner or edge so everyone is placed evenly around the perimeter. Then have everyone toss their stuffed animals onto the sheet.

Players bounce the sheet up and down, like a parachute (the hole in the middle will make this easier) trying to pop each other's stuffed animals off the sheet while keeping their own on. The winner is the one whose animal stays on the sheet the longest.

HOOK AND LOOP FASTENERS (AKA VELCRO)

HOOK-AND-LOOP FASTENERS ARE, in my book, one of the cleverest modern inventions, and you can use the self-adhesive kind to create these groovy games.

FACTS ABOUT HOOK-AND-LOOP FASTENERS

- Hook-and-loop fasteners is the generic name for what most of us call Velcro, which is a brand name (kind of like how we call tissues Kleenex or photocopies Xeroxes).
- George de Mestral, a Swiss man, invented Velcro in 1948 after studying how burrs clung to his hunting clothes.
- The word *Velcro* is a combination of the French words *velour* (a kind of soft fabric) and *crochet* (a process of looping yarn with a hook).
- One side of the fasteners are shaped like tiny stiff hooks; the other side is covered with teeny soft loops. When the two sides are pressed together, the hooks attach to the loops.

CATCH AND RELEASE

Here is a fun way to learn to play catch because the ball sticks to the mitt.

■■■ **PLAYERS** 2 or more

MATERIALS FOR 2 PLAYERS ■■■■■■■■■
■ 2 large plastic lids (6 to 8 inches in diameter) ■ 2 wide rubber bands (3 to 4 inches long) ■ marker ■ ruler ■ utility knife*
■ clear packing tape ■ ½-inch wide self-adhesive hook and loop fastener strips (2 feet) ■ scissors ■ 1 plastic baseball (aka Wiffle ball)

*Utility knives are *very* sharp and should be handled only by adults.

▶ Prep Work

To make a mitt, turn a plastic lid upside down and center the rubber band across the middle. Make a mark at each end of the rubber band. From these marks, draw a straight line up 1 inch, then connect those lines across. Use your utility knife to cut along the lines you've drawn to make a 1-inch rectangular flap.

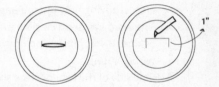

Flip the lid over (as if you were going to put the lid on a container) and slip the rubber band over the flap. Replace the flap and cover it with clear packing tape.

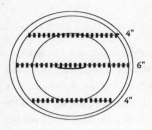

Next, turn the lid upside down again. Measure the distance across the inside of the lid in 3 places (top, middle, bottom) then cut strips of hook and loop fastener to those lengths. Separate the fastener into the fuzzy side and the grippy side. Cut the fuzzy side into strips to fit the 3 places on the lid, then remove the adhesive backing and press them onto the lid. Repeat these steps to make the second mitt.

To make the ball, wrap one of the grippy pieces of fastener around the center of the ball to get the correct length. Trim the strip, remove the adhesive backing, wrap it around the ball again and press firmly so that it sticks. Measure the correct length for 2 strips perpendicular to the first strip. Remove the backing and attach these strips to the ball.

▶ How to Play

Players slip a hand through the rubber-band strap on a mitt.

Now play catch with your friend!

BULL'S-EYE

*You'll need the most rudimentary sewing skills to make this project, but wait . . .
don't turn the page if sewing's not your thing. Seriously, if you can thread a
needle and sew on a button, you'll be able to make this. And, hear me out, this
is a great first sewing project if you've never been inclined to pick up a needle
and thread. Okay, okay, if you really loathe sewing, check your local craft supply
store for adhesive-backed felt squares, then stick instead of sew. In the end you'll
have a really fun indoor dart game that won't put anybody's eye out.*

■■■ **PLAYERS** 1 or more

MATERIALS

■ 1 9-inch plate ■ pencil or chalk ■ 1 2-inch plastic food container
lid ■ 2 squares of light-colored felt (adhesive-backed if you don't
sew; 12 inches by 12 inches) ■ 1 6-inch plate ■ 2 squares of dark-
colored felt (adhesive-backed if you don't sew; 12 inches by 12 inches)
■ scissors ■ 4 straight pins ■ sewing needle ■ thread (to match
the felt squares) ■ 2 thin black chenille stems (aka pipe cleaners; 12
inches long) ■ permanent black marker ■ wire hanger ■ 6 safety
pins (1 inch long) ■ 3 Ping-Pong balls ■ ½-inch-wide self-adhesive
hook and loop fastener strips (30 inches)

▶ Prep Work

First, trace the 9-inch plate
and the 2-inch lid on the light-
colored felt squares. Then trace
the 6-inch plate on a dark-
colored felt square. Cut out
these 3 circles.

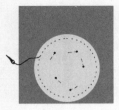

Use straight pins to place the 9-inch circle on the 12-inch dark-colored fabric square (so that the bottom of the circle nearly lines up with the bottom of the square). Thread your needle with the light-colored thread and sew on the 9-inch circle and remove the straight pins.

Pin the 6-inch circle in the center of the 9-inch circle and sew it on with needle and thread. Then do this for the 2-inch circle in the center of the 6-inch circle. Now you will have a bull's-eye pattern alternating dark and light felt.

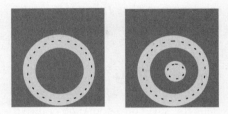

Cut 3½-inch lengths of chenille stem. Place one in the 12 o'clock position beginning at the top of the largest circle and ending at the top of the smallest circle. Attach the stem with 3 stitches at the top then 3 stitches at the bottom. Repeat this process with stems placed at 3 o'clock, 6 o'clock, and 9 o'clock.

Now, use a permanent black marker to write point values in each quadrant you've created as shown. (Of course, the super crafty may want to embroider the numbers or cut them out of the contrasting felt and sew them on. The rest of us could cut them out of adhesive-backed felt and stick them on.)

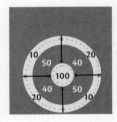

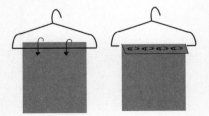

Flip the target over and position the bottom of the wire hanger 1 inch from the top of the dark-colored fabric square. Fold the flap of felt over the hanger and secure it with safety pins from one end to the other.

Next, make the balls. Wrap a strip of the grippy side of the hook and loop fastener tape around a Ping-Pong ball to get the correct length. Trim the strip, remove the adhesive backing, and wrap it around the ball again. Press down to secure. Then repeat this process to make 2 more strips perpendicular to the first one. Do the same for the other 2 balls.

▶ How to Play

Hang the target on a doorknob or turn the hook of the hanger 90 degrees and hang the target over the back of a chair (for little kids). For bigger kids, hang it over the back of a door.

Determine a throwing line (3 to 5 feet from the target, depending on the age and ability of players). Players take turns standing with toes on the line and throwing the balls toward the target. Add up points for any balls that stick. The player with the highest point total wins.

HUMAN BULL'S-EYE

Make no-sew felt vests (or try the sewn version) to turn you and your friends into moving targets for this high-energy, low-impact dodgeball game.

▪▪▪ **PLAYERS** 2 or more

MATERIALS
▪ felt (⅓ to ½ yard per vest)* ▪ ruler or measuring tape ▪ white chalk ▪ scissors ▪ safety pins ▪ ½-inch-wide self-adhesive hook-and-loop fastener tape (12 inches per ball) ▪ 3 Ping-Pong balls per player

*The directions are for 36-inch-wide felt. Some fabric stores sell 72-inch-wide felt; if that's what you buy you should be able to get 2 vests out of ½ yard.

▶ **Prep Work**

Use the measurements shown to determine the correct size for your players.

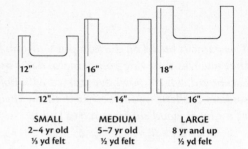

SMALL
2–4 yr old
⅓ yd felt

MEDIUM
5–7 yr old
½ yd felt

LARGE
8 yr and up
½ yd felt

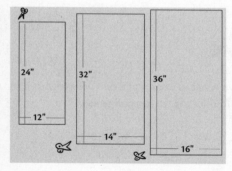

For each vest, lay the felt on a flat, safe cutting surface. Measure, mark (with white chalk), and cut out a rectangle of fabric using the correct dimensions for the size vest you want to make.

Fold the rectangle of fabric in half so the short sides meet. Measure, mark (with white chalk), and cut out a rounded rectangular shape from the top center of the fabric using the head hole dimensions for the size of your vest.

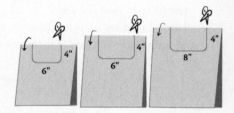

From the head hole piece you just cut out, cut four 1-inch-wide strips of fabric.

Use safety pins to attach the strips of fabric centered on the left and right panels of the front and back of the vests.

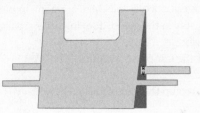

To make the balls, wrap a strip of the grippy side of the hook and loop fastener tape around a Ping-Pong ball to get the correct length. Trim the strip, remove the adhesive backing, and wrap it around the ball again. Press down to secure. Then repeat this process to make 2 more strips perpendicular to the first one. Do the same for the other 2 balls.

▶ How to Play

Simple Version: Determine the boundaries of your playing field, then give each player a vest to wear plus 3 grippy Ping-Pong balls. Players follow these rules:

1. Players run around the field, throwing balls at one another, trying to land them on the vests of their opponents.
2. Once players have 3 balls stuck to their vest, they must remove the balls, toss them to the ground, and sit outside the boundaries of the field.

3. Any player can snatch balls on the ground and use them against opponents.

4. If a player runs out of balls and there are none to pick up off the ground, he or she can stay in the game, dodging others' balls, until 3 balls get stuck to the vest.

5. The winner is the last person without 3 balls on his or her vest.

Super Version: To step up the game, make felt bull's-eye targets on the vests.

ADDITIONAL MATERIALS

■ squares of felt in 2 contrasting colors (or a ¼ yard in 2 different colors; 12 inches by 12 inches)* ■ scissors ■ 1 9-inch plate ■ 1 6-inch plate ■ 1 2-inch lid ■ straight pins ■ needle ■ thread (in colors to match the felt)

---

*If you really loathe sewing, check your local craft store for adhesive-backed felt squares. Then follow the directions, but instead of stitching your target together, just stick it!

For each vest, trace the 9-inch plate and the 2-inch lid on the light-color felt. Then trace the 6-inch plate on a dark-color felt square. Cut out these 3 circles. Then repeat so you have 2 of each circle.

Use straight pins to center the 9-inch circle on the front of the vest. Thread your needle with the light color and sew on the 9-inch circle then remove the straight pins.

Pin the 6-inch circle in the center of the 9-inch circle and sew it on with needle and thread. Then do this for the 2-inch circle in the center of the 6-inch circle. Now you will have a bull's-eye pattern alternating in dark- and light-color felt on the front of the vest. Repeat to make a bull's-eye pattern on the back of the vest.

FRONT   BACK

▶ How to Play

Determine the boundaries of your playing field then give each player a vest to wear and 3 grippy Ping-Pong balls. Players must follow these rules:

1. Players run around the field, throwing balls at one another, trying to land them on a bull's-eye target on their opponents' vests.
2. Any balls that land outside the target may be removed by the player wearing the vest and used on an opponent.
3. Once a player has 3 balls stuck to his or her target, that player must remove the balls, toss them to the ground, and sit outside the boundaries of the field.
4. Any player can snatch the balls on the ground and use them against opponents.
5. If you run out of your own balls and there are none on the ground to pick up, you can stay in the game, dodging others' balls as long as you don't have 3 balls stuck to your target.
6. The winner is the last person without 3 balls stuck to the front or back of his or her bull's-eye.

EXTRA FUN
◆ Make the belted beanbag carriers from Beanbag Tag on page 29 plus more balls for each player. Play the Super Version but allow players to stow their balls inside the carrier.

15 VARIATIONS OF TAG

WHAT GAME BOOK would be complete without variations of the quickest, easiest, best game ever? Tag is as old as the hills and played the world over, but if you're tired of the same old game, check out all these variations. Now go outside already!

No matter the version, the basic rules of Tag stay the same:

1. Determine the boundaries of your playing field.

2. Decide if you want to have a base (a safe place where players can't be tagged, such as a tree) and decide how long players can stay on base before they have to move (usually about 5 seconds).

SCISSORS

3. Use your favorite "You Are Not It" game to decide who will be It first.

PAPER   ROCK

4. The person who is It chases all the other players around the playing field trying to tag them.

5. Agree on whether there are tag-backs or no tag-backs. Tag-backs means the person who is tagged can immediately tag It back. No tag-backs means the person who is tagged must tag someone other the one who was just It.

TAG BACKS   NO TAG BACKS

Now let's see how many ways there are to play Tag.

+ **TAG YOU'RE IT:** The person who gets tagged becomes the new It and the person who was It becomes a regular player.

+ **TAG YOU'RE OUT:** The person who gets tagged is out and must sit on the sidelines. When everyone is out, the last person tagged becomes It for the next round.

+ **INFECTION TAG:** Every person tagged joins It and tries to tag more people. The last person tagged starts as the first It in the next round.

+ **SHADOW TAG:** Instead of touching the other players, the person who is It must step on players' shadows.

◆ **CARTOON TAG:** Players can avoid being tagged by squatting down and yelling out the name of a cartoon character. Players can stay in the squatting position for only 3 seconds. Players may not repeat a cartoon character that has been shouted by any other player. Of course, less TV-minded individuals could choose to play with book characters, fruits and veggies, or 19th-century German art song composers instead.

◆ **HOSPITAL TAG:** A player must place one hand over the area of his or her body that is tagged as if bleeding from a wound. For example, if a player is tagged on the shoulder, he must hold one hand on his shoulder and continue to run around. The second time a player is tagged, he must place his other hand on that place. (For example, if he is tagged on his knee, he will now have to run with one hand holding his shoulder and one hand holding his knee). If that player is tagged a third time, he becomes It.

◆ **FREEZE TAG:** Any player who is tagged must freeze on the field until another player tags them to set them free. Play until all players are frozen. The last player to be frozen is the new It.

◆ **STATUE TAG:** Just like Freeze Tag only when players are tagged they have to freeze in the exact position they were tagged in and stay in that position until another player tags them to set them free.

- **STUCK-IN-THE MUD TAG:** Another version of Freeze Tag but frozen people have to stand with their legs wide apart and can be unfrozen only when another player crawls between their legs.

- **TOILET TAG:** In this hilarious (if you find potty humor funny, that is . . .) version of Freeze Tag, the frozen players must kneel down on one knee and stick one arm out to the side. They can be unfrozen only when another player comes along and flushes them by pushing their arm down.

- **PAIR TAG:** Choose 1 person to be It and another person to be the Runner. Everyone else finds a partner and links arms, then the pairs stand in a big circle. It chases the Runner who can

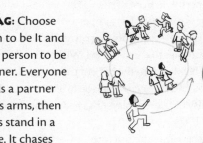

go around the circle or weave in and out while trying to link arms with a standing player before being tagged by It. If the runner successfully links arms, then the third person (the one in the pair not chosen by the Runner) must peel off and become the Runner being chased by It. If It tags the Runner before he or she can link arms with another person, then the Runner becomes It.

- **BLOB TAG:** Choose 2 people to be It. They hold hands as the Blob and chase the others. If the Blob tags someone, that person becomes part of the Blob and must hold hands with one person in the Blob. Keep playing until everyone is part of the Blob.

IT   TAGS   NEW IT

- **DEAD ANT TAG:** When players are tagged in this game, they must fall to their backs and stick their arms and legs in the air (like a dead ant). To be rescued, 4 other players must carry the dead ant by the arms and legs outside the boundaries of the playing field to be revived.  Rescuers cannot be tagged while they are rescuing another player. As soon as the dead ant crosses the boundary, all 5 players must go back on the field again.

- **DRAGON TAIL TAG:** Players stand in a line and hold the shoulders of the person in front of them. The first person in the line is the head. The last person in the line is the tail. With everyone holding on and staying in line, the head tries to catch the tail. When the tail is caught, the head goes to the back of the line to become the tail and the second person in line  becomes the head. Play until every player has had a chance to be the head.

- **OCTOPUS TAG:** In this game the fish (the players), must move from one side of the ocean (the playing field) to the other while the octopus (the person who is It) stands in the center and calls out commands, then tries to tag as many fish as possible. For example the octopus calls, "Come run [jump, hop on 1 leg, walk backward, etc.] across my ocean." The fish must move  across the ocean the way the octopus says while the octopus tags as many fish as possible. All the fish who get tagged turn to seaweed and stay where they are in the ocean as obstacles to the other fish. Any fish that make it to the other side are safe. Then the octopus turns around to face the fish and calls another way to get across. Play until the last fish is tagged, then that player becomes the new octopus and all the fish join in again.

GLOSSARY

BAMBOO SKEWER: thin 12- to 18-inch pointed wooden stick used to make shish kababs

C-CLAMP (G-CLAMP): a metal C-shaped clamp with a long screw used to hold two things together, found in hardware stores

CANNING JAR LID RINGS: metal replacement rings for screw-top canning jars (sold wherever you can buy canning supplies)

CHENILLE STEM (PIPE CLEANER): a long wire covered with short, soft polyester bristles

CRAFT STICK (TONGUE DEPRESSOR OR POPSICLE STICK): flat wooden stick with rounded ends that comes in many sizes and colors

FELT: a type of fabric that doesn't fray, comes in 12-inch squares, and can be bought by the yard

FOAM BOARD (FOAM CORE): a layer of foam that's been laminated on both sides

PUSHPIN: a pin with a ¼-inch plastic head over a small sharp nail; unlike a thumbtack, which has a flat head

SCORING (CARDBOARD OR FOAM BOARD): using one blade of scissors or a utility knife, cut only halfway through the material so the board will fold

SELF-ADHESIVE HOOK AND LOOP FASTENER (VELCRO): two-part fastener that comes in different shapes and sizes; look for the words *self-adhesive* on the packaging

SPOOL: a flanged cylinder (usually plastic or wood) that thread is wrapped around

TYVEK ENVELOPES: envelopes made of spunbond olefin, the sturdy material used for Express Mail envelopes by the U.S. Postal Service

UTILITY KNIFE (BOX CUTTER, CARPET KNIFE): sharp 3- to 4-inch razor blade held in a plastic or metal casing

WAX PAPER: food wrap sold in rolls found with the plastic wrap and aluminum foil

INDEX